CANDIDATE

FOR

C
A
E

**FIONA
JOSEPH**
+
**PETER
TRAVIS**

TEACHER'S BOOK

**PHOENIX
ELT**

incorporating
PRENTICE HALL MACMILLAN

New York   London   Toronto   Sydney   Tokyo   Singapore

First published 1996 by
Phoenix ELT
A division of Prentice Hall International
Campus 400, Spring Way,
Maylands Avenue,
Hemel Hempstead,
Hertfordshire, HP2 7EZ

Designed by Robert Wheeler
Printed and bound in Great Britain by
Redwood Books, Trowbridge, Wiltshire

British Library Cataloguing-in-Publication Data
A catalogue record of this book is available from
the British Library

ISBN   0-13-305624-4

5 4 3 2 1
1999 98 97 96

Contents

Student's Book Contents

Vocabulary development	Pronunciation	Exploring language	Language Awareness
Phrases for giving advice Terminology	Helping yourself to improve	Common grammatical errors	Improving grammar
Common expressions using 'as … as' Language of discussing		**Exam Focus: discourse cloze**	Dependent prepositions Questions (1)
Ways of getting around			Language of obligation Reported speech
Common expressions connected with health	Word stress	**Exam Focus: proofreading**	Defining and non-defining relative clauses Passive or active?
Words for talking about language Guessing unknown words	Pronunciation of marker words	**Exam Focus: informal to formal writing**	Formal and informal language Expressing time
Food collocations Using synonyms in writing Recording vocabulary	Vowel sounds		Participles (1) Expressing possibility

	Reading	Writing	Speaking	Listening
7 **The Human Condition** *page* 76	Article on memorising: •skimming •specific information	Article for a newsletter	Giving descriptions	3 adults who were gifted children: •global understanding •specific information and inference **Exam Focus:** **gap fill**
8 **Leisure** *page* 87	Book and film reviews: •skimming •scanning and inferring A visit to Alton Towers: •appreciating the writer's tone	Language of reviews **Exam Focus:** **letter of complaint**	Viewing and reading habits **Exam Focus:** **describing photographs**	**Exam Focus:** **identifying topics and opinions** 2 learners practise for paper 5: •specific information
9 **Human Relationships** *page* 98	Couples in crisis: •skimming Article on types of love: •predicting •comprehension	Magazine article Reply to a problem page	Parenting **Exam Focus:** **information gap**	Extract from a love letter: •global understanding •specific information
10 **Work** *page* 109	**Exam Focus:** **multiple matching**	**Exam Focus:** **a letter to a friend**	Choosing a career Trade unions	Interview with a dancer: •specific information Account of psychometric testing: •specific information
11 **Power Relationships** *page* 121	Article on assassination: •identifying paragraph topics **Exam Focus:** **multiple choice** Description of life in Trikeri: •scanning •inference Newspaper extracts: •scanning	Account for an encyclopaedia Formal report	Male and female roles Role play	Extracts from a radio show: •global understanding **Exam Focus:** **gap-fill**
12 **Crime and Punishment** *page* 134	Articles on smacking children: •global understanding •appreciating the style of a text **Exam Focus:** **paragraph cloze**	**Exam Focus:** **a letter to a newspaper**	Types of crime Fear of crime	**Exam Focus:** **identifying topics and speakers** Advice from a Crime Prevention Officer: •specific information

Vocabulary development	Pronunciation	Exploring language	Language Awareness
Collocations Word-building (roots and affixes)		**Exam focus:** **proofreading**	Verb forms (1) 'Will', 'would' and 'used to'
Vocabulary to describe books, films and TV	Ways of improving fluency	Punctuation marks	Questions (2) Future forms
Describing personal characteristics Emotions		**Exam Focus:** **discourse cloze**	Conditionals Past forms
Common colloquial expressions Common abbreviations	Pronunciation of connected speech	**Exam Focus:** **lexical cloze** **and open cloze** **Exam Focus:** **expanding from notes**	Verb forms (2) Participles (2)
Guessing unknown words Opposites Homophones		**Exam focus: open cloze**	Emphatic structures Multi-word verbs
Types of crime Synonyms	Pronunciation in word families		Perfect tenses Articles

Introduction

Welcome to *Candidate for* CAE Teacher's Book. In this book you will find:

- a complete description of activities in the Student's Book
- an answer key to all tasks in the Student's Book
- useful extension activities and ideas for you to adapt the material here.

How *Candidate for* CAE is organised

Candidate for CAE is divided into 12 units, each with a global theme (for example, language, personal relationships, work). Each unit contains three sub-topics of around three pages to provide a regular change of focus and to make the material easier to use. A typical unit provides around 10 hours of teaching material and has the following components:

- systematic training in the four skills as well as vocabulary development, language exploration and pronunciation exercises
- a stimulating montage of images on the opening pages of each unit, which can be exploited for vocabulary-building purposes
- two Language Awareness pages at the end of the unit to enhance learners' understanding of major grammatical structures
- at least two Exam Focus sections per unit to provide practice in each CAE question type
- a Review page at the end of every unit for learners to reflect on and record what they have done.

In addition *Candidate for* CAE Student's Book offers:

- a Writing Skills Development section with sample student essays and guidance for learners on how to evaluate their work
- tapescripts for all recorded material
- a Grammar Reference which gives a commentary on all the language points in each unit.

Key principles

Candidate for CAE has been written with the following principles and beliefs in mind:

- We should respect the learner and not expect him or her to do activities that we would find boring or patronising ourselves.

- Learners learn most effectively through discovering language rules for themselves rather than being told at the outset.
- Learners should have an explicit knowledge of the language itself as well as being able to communicate effectively in the language. Terms such as 'skimming', 'collocation', 'cloze', 'word stress', etc. should be part of the learner's own language.
- The most effective learners are those who are willing to invest in and take at least some responsibility for their own learning. Over-dependence on a coursebook or teacher is not desirable. We believe that learners should be encouraged to reflect on what they have learned and to plan their own learning outside the classroom.
- Learning materials should respect the learner's own culture and offer important opportunities for the learner to respond from his or her own perspective.
- An examination textbook should inspire confidence in both the teacher and the learner.
- A coursebook should be seen as a springboard to learning.

Meeting the needs of examination students

This book has been written specifically to meet the needs of learners preparing for the Certificate in Advanced English (CAE). It can also be used with non-examination students who merely wish to improve their language skills to an advanced level in order to communicate effectively in the real world.

Language exam students need to have specific knowledge and language skills:

- to have reached the required level of language proficiency in English as described by the examining board
- to be entirely familiar with the examination format
- to understand the rationale for each exam question
- to be able to perform tasks within a specified time limit.

In order to meet these needs, *Candidate for* CAE has 22 Exam Focus sections that give systematic practice in each of the exam questions for all five papers. Each Exam Focus question is presented in a form that mirrors that of a real exam question (with similar layout and rubrics). However, there is clear learner training in that students are guided through the question in a series of stages, with useful tips for approaching that particular question type. By the end of the book, your students should be thoroughly familiar with the format of the CAE exam. Of course, towards the end of the year they will benefit from using practice tests or past papers in the final stage of preparing for the exam.

What follows is a description of and rationale for the activities in the Student's Book. We recommend that you read this section before you start teaching.

Reading

Tasks

In *Candidate for* CAE there are 24 main reading texts that come from a variety of authentic sources, such as British newspapers, magazines (both general and specific interest), leaflets, books (academic, popular fiction) and advertisements. These texts have been chosen to cover a wide range of writing functions (to inform, to amuse, to surprise and so on) as well as a variety of topics. Authenticity has been a key issue in English language teaching for many years, and remains so, not least because learners can be given exposure to 'real' language in use rather than that which is contrived or made-up.

The reading activities are designed to train learners in the intensive reading techniques of scanning and skimming that are essential for the CAE exam but are also practical, real-life reading skills. Reading tasks are in a variety of formats, such as true/false, multiple matching, multiple choice and general comprehension questions. It is also crucial for you to encourage your students to read quickly and efficiently.

Methodology

1 As a general approach, tasks that ask learners to read for a general understanding are usually presented first. In order to promote speed reading, a number of these tasks will have a 'clock' symbol and a recommended time limit for learners to complete the task.

2 Learners read a second time in closer detail, to obtain specific information, to infer meaning/attitude or to complete a task, for example.

3 The text may then be exploited for follow-up vocabulary work to be discussed in pairs or groups.

Further practice

Obviously, no coursebook alone can ever provide sufficient extensive reading practice for learners. If you are teaching in Britain or a country where English is one of the official languages, you will have access to a number of up-to-date sources of authentic material (from CD-ROM, libraries, tourist information, local and national press). You can use any of these to supplement the reading texts in this book, but do bear in mind the copyright laws. Better still, ask your students to collect their own texts according to their personal interests.

If you are in a teaching context where English is not an official language, it will be harder for you to supplement your students' reading. However, novels in English are an excellent source for extensive reading for pleasure. At this level, learners should be guided towards books in their authentic form rather than graded readers.

Writing

Tasks

In *Candidate for* CAE there are 23 writing tasks that cover a wide range of writing types, including reports and articles, competition entries, reviews, letters (formal and informal), leaflets and problem page replies. The majority of tasks have an authentic purpose, and all of them are set between 200 and 300 words to conform to the word limit of CAE. Obviously, you may choose to set your students extended pieces of writing in addition to the writing tasks.

Methodology

All of the writing tasks give extensive attention to the process of writing, as follows:

1 Small groups can work together to brainstorm for ideas regarding the content of the piece of writing. Learners are also asked to consider the purpose of the task, the audience for whom they are writing and the style of writing that is appropriate to the task.

2 Learners usually write a first draft in class (individually) which can then be followed by focused peer comment or teacher feedback. Attention to organisation is also necessary at this stage.

3 Learners can write a final draft outside the classroom in which careful and appropriate presentation and thorough proofreading (to tie in with English in Use, Section B) are of paramount importance. We find it useful to encourage typed work from our students.

5 Final feedback may come from you, the teacher, and/or other students.

6 Optional stage: 'Publication' of students' work can be highly motivating. The term can be used loosely to describe photocopying work for other students to read or having class displays or magazines.

(See Hedge, 1987 or White and Arndt, 1989 for a more detailed discussion of the process of writing.)

Formal feedback

If you are preparing your students for CAE, then you may want to use the marking criteria from UCLES to assess their work. There are, however, many ways to vary the way in which feedback may be given to your students:

- Give back written work with errors indicated but not corrected.
- Collect recurrent errors from a number of scripts and distribute them to the students for whole class correction.
- For writing tasks that have an intended publication (for example, the letter to a newspaper, Unit 12; problem page replies, Units 1 and 9), you can ask your students to work in groups acting as editors and choosing the best piece of writing for publication. (We would like to thank Mark Searle of Exeter Academy for this idea, suggested during piloting of the material.)

Further writing skills development

At the back of the Student's Book you will find a section called Writing Skills Development, which is a further source of exploitation for writing practice. This section has been written to train learners in how to correct each other's work and their own. There are five sample essays, all of which have come from our own students, for them to practise on. You will realise that each of the sample essays is in response to a writing task from a particular unit. Your students are advised not to look at the sample answer (which is by no means always a correct model) until they have completed their own version.

Listening

Tasks

There are 23 main listening tasks; these are primarily monologues, interviews and conversations. The texts are either completely authentic or semi-authentic (recorded by actors for the sake of quality). We have found that authentic material of the more formal, planned type such as a radio interview or speech is much easier for learners to cope with than the typical conversational discourse of two native speakers in a pub!

Methodology

1 Most texts have activities which require learners to listen to the tape twice.
2 They will listen the first time usually to perform a task which requires global understanding only; for example, ticking main points.
3 At the second listening, they have more detailed information to find, and need to fill in a chart or make notes.

4 As a follow-up, there is pair or group comparison of ideas.

Note that listening tasks towards the end of the book can be completed under exam conditions.

Speaking

Tasks

Speaking skills are covered by a variety of tasks. Each sub-section within a unit has its own lead-in designed to encourage discussion and sharing of ideas. There are clearly labelled 'Speaking skill' activities which put an emphasis on a specific skill, such as sharing opinions and reaching agreement, or the more formal skills of debating or role play, which require preparation. At any time, however, learners should be given the opportunity to respond to the material presented. Of the four skills, it is speaking that can be most easily integrated within a lesson.

Methodology

Learners can and should be encouraged to speak as much as possible. We are not against using the native language in the classroom *per se*, but it makes clear sense at this level for the lesson to be managed in English.

Emphasis is placed on pair and small group work throughout the course; for example, many of the activities ask learners to exchange their answers, trying to justify their own responses if they differ from their partner's. This should be encouraged for a number of reasons:

- It gives learners a chance to enjoy using English in a non-threatening situation.
- It ensures that everybody has a chance to speak.
- It improves general fluency.
- It encourages skills of interaction and co-operation needed for the Speaking paper.

Feedback

As with writing, there are various ways that you can give your students feedback. We have found that in fluency-focused activities it is best to wait until the speaking is over before you give correction on errors. Do not forget to praise as well!

Student feedback can be organised by having one student to monitor a particular speaking activity and to focus on paralinguistic factors such as body language or tone of voice.

Pronunciation

Pronunciation is treated as a separate area in *Candidate for* CAE. There are a number of pronunciation tasks that serve as awareness-raising activities; for example, contrasting vowel and consonant sounds, or word stress and intonation. If you teach a monolingual class, you will find that many of your students share the same pronunciation problems. In this case you can adapt the activity to suit your students. We recommend that the International Phonetic Alphabet (IPA) is used as an integral part of pronunciation activities. In the first unit, 'Starting off', there is an introduction to using the IPA. If you are not familiar with the pronunciation problems of particular nationalities, we have found that Kenworthy (1987) and Swan and Smith (1987) are excellent points of reference.

Vocabulary

Tasks
Vocabulary development in *Candidate for* CAE is presented in three forms:

- highlighting of particular vocabulary items after a text has been read
- theme-related vocabulary
- common vocabulary classifications, such as homophones, antonyms and idioms.

In addition, many of the writing tasks have key phrases that learners will find useful during the writing stage.

Methodology
1 Learners will benefit from learning the metalanguage (i.e. language for talking about language) of English. This includes not only key grammatical terminology ('noun', 'verb', 'participle', 'tense') but also terms such as 'collocation', 'synonym' and 'colloquial language', which are also presented explicitly.
2 Use of these terms should aid learners in developing their own methods for classifying and recording vocabulary.
3 Many of the activities assume that students have access to a good monolingual advanced learner's dictionary.
4 In reading a text, learners are encouraged to develop vocabulary-guessing strategies by making full use of the context.
5 Learners should remember set phrases or chunks of language as well as individual words (Lewis, 1993).

Language awareness

Tasks
There are 23 Language Awareness sections, which are always located at the end of the unit. Most major grammatical structures expected of learners at this level are covered. For the benefit of the students, there is a Grammar Reference section at the back of the Student's Book that allows the students to answer the questions in the Language Awareness section.

We suggest that the Language Awareness sections are dealt with at the points indicated in the Student's Book (for example 'See Language Awareness: questions (1)' on page 19). This allows for a good balance during the lesson between skills practice and language work. In some cases, indicated in the teacher's notes, the Language Awareness section is specifically linked to a subsequent activity.

Methodology
1 The fundamental principle of these activities is that learners are guided to discover for themselves grammatical forms and their usages. (See Bolitho and Tomlinson, 1980.)
2 Learners arrive at their answers by analysing the language data, and are often required to make certain decisions based on their prior knowledge of the particular structure. They then check their answers with the teacher or in the Grammar Reference.
3 Language is presented in a variety of motivating contexts: puzzles, letters, short newspaper articles, listening texts, sentence level examples of usage or extracts from previous texts.

References
T. Hedge (1987) *Writing*, OUP
R. White & V. Arndt (1989) *Process Writing*, Longman
J. Kenworthy (1987) *Teaching English Pronunciation*, Longman
M. Swan & B.Smith eds (1987) *Learner English*, CUP
M. Lewis (1993) *The Lexical Approach*, LTP
R. Bolitho and B. Tomlinson (1980) *Discover English*, Heinemann

Starting Off

The aims of this unit are for the students to get to know each other (and you, if appropriate), to reflect on their own experiences of learning English, to learn some key terminology, and to become familiar with the different elements of the CAE exam.

PART ONE
Getting to know each other (SB page 6)

You may be using this book in one of the following situations:

a This is the first time that you and your students have met.
b This is your first time with the class although they already know each other (this commonly happens in monolingual classes).
c You and the students have worked together before at a previous level and/or with another textbook.

Each situation is slightly different so we suggest that you adapt this activity as is appropriate.

Lead-in

This first section contains some 'getting to know you' questions designed to help the students find out more about each other and to feel at ease during the first session using the book.

1 Allow at least 10 minutes for the students to think about these questions on their own, as they require a depth of personal response. When they seem to have finished, put them into small groups (depending on your class size) to share this information with others. The students will probably find it fun if you join in too! As an option, you can get the students to introduce a colleague to the whole class and explain one of their answers.

2 After Activity 1 the students should be nicely 'warmed up'. Ask them to write down the one aspect of studying English they find the most frustrating and give the piece of paper to you. Shuffle all the papers and redistribute them. Tell the students they have to find the owner of their piece of paper.

Extension activity

At the start of the lesson give all the students a copy of a letter that you have written about yourself. Things to include might be:

- personal details (e.g. your age, family details)
- how long you have been teaching
- your hobbies and interests
- what you expect from them as a class (e.g. punctuality, agreement to use English whenever possible)

As a first homework activity ask each member of the group to write a similar letter back to you which echoes the points you have made in your letter. This will give you a useful idea from an early stage of their writing ability in English, as well as giving you a more rounded idea of the students as individuals.

Reading technique: skimming

1 This is the first reading activity in the book and aims to practise skimming skills. Students read the letters and tick those problems which are similar to the ones they discussed in the lead-in.

2 Students discuss suitable replies for each of these problem page letters and this then leads to whole class discussion on typical problems of learners. This is a point at which you can offer them good advice based on your experience as a teacher. Try to let them come up with their own ideas, however. We suggest that you use the board for writing down their suggestions. In our experience, students are incredibly imaginative, even if they don't always follow their own advice.

3 As a conclusion, students can discuss any problems that were not covered by the selection of letters in the problem page.

Vocabulary development: phrases for giving advice

This activity focuses on the accuracy of common phrases for making suggestions/giving advice. If students are unfamiliar with the grammatical terminology, put the following example on the board.

a -ing (going)
b bare infinitive (go)
c to + infinitive (to go)

Let students work together in pairs.

Answers

- what about + a
- you ought + c
- you'd better + b
- have you considered + a (a common mistake is for students to use c)
- why don't you + b
- I'd advise you + c (Students commonly use b)
- you could always + b
- it might be a good idea + c
- I suggest you + b (Students also have prob lems with this structure – they tend to use c by mistake; cf. I suggest + a)
- if I were you, I'd + b

Encourage students to learn off by heart a few of these expressions as set phrases .

Writing skill: a reply to a problem page

1 Students work together in this activity. Group writing tasks can be valuable for encouraging co-operation and negotiation between students. All group members should contribute ideas for the letter, with one member acting as secretary while the others dictate the contents.

2 Get students to swap letters and comment on the advice given (was it useful, practical etc.?) and the language used (was it grammatically accurate with a friendly tone?). If you like you can ask them to give marks out of ten for each.

Suggestion: Photocopy the letters for the whole class.

Exploring language: common grammatical errors

1 Having read some of the other students' letters and judging from their own personal experience, students discuss common grammatical errors made by learners at this level. Encourage them to make a list of types of mistakes. Common ones tend to be:

- incorrect prepositions of time and place
- incorrect dependent prepositions
- absence of third person -s in present tense regular verbs
- lack of verb agreement
- incorrect vocabulary choice

2 Students now read the other letters and see if any of the mistakes they have listed appear in

those letters. Now would be a good time to introduce the students to the skill of proof-reading – explain its importance for the English in Use paper, Section B.

PART TWO
You the language learner (SB page 9)

Lead-in

This section continues and expands on the theme of the language learner. To stimulate discussion as well as to raise anticipation for the listening, students must respond to the listed points. Ask them to modify any statements they are not in total agreement with.

Listening technique: global understanding

Students listen to a recording of three adult students (two German, one Dutch) who have completed the final year of their business degrees at a British university. Students listen and put the appropriate number next to each statement in the Lead-in.

Answers

Extract 1 = f
       2 = b
       3 = d
       4 = e
       5 = c
       6 = a

Listening technique: specific information

1 Students listen and make notes while you play the tape for the second time.

Suggested answers

Vocabulary
They feel their vocabulary didn't increase that much over the year; different viewpoints of vocabulary learning: writing new words down versus using them in real situations (Extract 6).

Reading
Reading helps writing by reinforcing new words and expressions (Extract 2); you become more fluent in reading with practice and have less need to rely on a dictionary all the time (Extract 3).

Writing
Writing is improved by reading a lot and using similar expressions that you read or hear (Extract 2); with practice you become more confident in writing essays (Extract 2).

Speaking/Pronunciation
Speaking has got better over time (Extract 1); you are able to express yourself more fluently and even if you don't know a particular word, you are able to describe it more successfully (Extract 1); you know you've pronounced a word incorrectly when (English) people begin to laugh at you (Extract 4).

(You should explain the difference between 'bowl' and 'bowel'!)

Listening
Listening is one of the easiest skills despite having to come to terms with various accents and dialects in Britain (Extract 1).

Grammar
Grammar is a weak point; speaking fluently is easy but not necessarily with correct grammar (Extract 1); they feel that grammar is hard to improve without constant correction from native speakers (Extract 4).

Allow students time to compare their answers. If you are teaching in Britain (particularly in a college or university), it may be interesting to conduct a whole class discussion on these points.

2 Ask students to reflect on their own abilities in each of these areas using the scale *good*, *average* or *weak* (or 5 to 1 if they need to be more precise). Again, you can allow time for group or whole class feedback.

Exploring pronunciation: helping yourself to improve

Start this particular activity by eliciting from the students how important correct pronunciation is to them. If you have a monolingual class then it will be relatively easy to identify pronunciation problems for your learners. Note that all of the words for these exercises have been chosen because in our experience as teachers we find them to be the most frequently mispronounced words.

First, familiarise your students with the phonetic symbols in the chart. These represent all the sounds in English and are numbered for ease of reference.

1 To begin with, students focus on vowel sounds and common problematic words. Students complete the chart as in the first example.

Answers

b	ill	(D)	/ɪ/
	I		/aɪ/
c	topic	(D)	/ɒ/
	total		/əʊ/
d	discuss	(S)	/ʌ/
	bus		/ʌ/
e	represent	(S)	/e/
	better		/e/
f	towards	(D)	/ɔ:/
	car		/ɑ:/
g	bought	(D)	/ɔ:/
	cough		/ɒ/
h	money	(D)	/i:/
	they		/eɪ/

When students are exchanging answers, they can indicate the number of the vowel sounds if they have real problems.

2
Answers

a	church	(D)	/tʃ/
	architecture		/k/
b	weather	(S)	/ð/
	clothes		/ð/

This might be a useful time to reinforce the correct pronunciation of 'clothes'.(/kləʊðz/)

| c | climb | (S) | /m/ |
| | bomb | | /m/ |

Both have silent 'b'

d	refrigerate	(D)	/dʒ/
	target		/g/
e	listen	(D)	/s/
	list		/st/
f	controversial	(D)	/ʃ/
	measure		/ʒ/
g	injured	(S)	/dʒ/
	jail		/dʒ/
h	knee	(D)	silent
	kettle		/k/

3 Word stress is a crucial part of pronunciation, and perhaps more important than individual vowel or consonant sounds. Most words with more than one syllable have a fixed stress pattern. Unfortunately, there are very few rules to help students know which particular syllable should be stressed. Your advice to students should be to record the stress pattern of any new words along with the definition/spelling. They can include this information in the way that dictionaries do (e.g. /kæpɪtl/)or, as we have done in this book with the symbol ⊏⊐ above the stressed syllable.

Divide students into two groups, A and B, in order for them to work on their list of words. Encourage group co-operation for this exercise and let them check their answers in a good monolingual dictionary if these are available.

Answers

Group A

identify   university

advertisement   problem

fashionable   logical

photography   fourteen

Group B

forty   unhappy

preposition   develop

information   experiment

consequence   wonderful

PART THREE
A candidate for CAE (SB page 11)

The main focus of this final part is on preparation for the exam and some final, useful learner training skills.

Lead-in

For this activity we have collected some of the most frequently asked questions about CAE, bearing in mind that the exam is still relatively new. Students who have taken First Certificate will already be familiar with the five-paper format. Put the students into pairs and check how much they already know about the exam.

Reading technique: scanning

Students read the description of the CAE exam and find the answers to the questions given and any others they may have. The final question, 'How can I prepare for the exam?', is usually the one which students are keenest to know the answer to. Reinforce the importance of students getting as much exposure to the language as possible, both in and outside the classroom. The next activity asks them to look through the Student's Book and to make a note of all the Exam Focus sections and their page numbers. We think that it's reassuring for students to know that their coursebook will contain systematic practice of exam type questions.

Reading technique: scanning

You can make this activity a light-hearted one by setting a time limit for its completion. Alternatively, you could put students in pairs with each of them looking for the page numbers in different halves of their book.

Answers

Reading

multiple choice 123	multiple matching 34, 116	sentence/ paragraph cloze 41, 140

Writing

Section A 94, 111	Section B 30, 69, 138

English in Use

Section A 113, 127	Section B 47, 56, 81	Section C 21, 99, 117

Listening

Section A 129	Section B 83	Section C 31	Section D 63, 87, 135

Speaking

Phase A –	Phase B 91, 105	Phase C 24	Phase D 24

Note that Phase A does not have extensive practice. This is the introductory phase of the Speaking paper and it is better that candidates sound natural and spontaneous. Therefore, discourage them from rehearsing set lines for this part.

Note also that many of the other activities are similar to those in the exam but have not been specifically labelled 'Exam Focus'.

Vocabulary development: terminology

This activity aims to teach students the key meta-language (i.e. language for talking about language) that will crop up in the classification of vocabulary for language learning purposes.

1 Get students to check their understanding of these terms to start with. Delay whole class feedback until Activity 2 has been completed. Don't expect 100 per cent knowledge of these terms!

2
Answers

> a synonym
> b antonym
> c idiom/expression
> d specialist
> e multi-word verb
> f root (happi-), affix (un-, -ness)
> g word family
> h homophone
> i collocation
> j compound
> k abbreviation
> l colloquialism

LANGUAGE AWARENESS:
improving grammar

This activity is included to show students how invaluable short authentic texts can be as a means of raising their language awareness.

1 Students read the article and discuss who deserves their support.

2 Students read the text again, this time looking for any interesting grammatical structures that appear frequently.

Suggested answers

> articles
> passives
> present perfect / past simple

3 Students work in pairs, one underlining all the indefinite articles, the other the definite articles. They can then work together and examine whether the use of these articles in the text is confirmed by the information in the Grammar Reference section.

4 Students now look specifically for the following:
  a the definite article used with a noun that has already been referred to
  b the definite article used when making reference to a unique noun
  c the indefinite article used with a countable singular noun referred to for the first time.

Answers

> The list is not exhaustive but is meant to provide examples of these uses. Articles are examined in greater depth in Unit 12.
>
> a the gift
>   the trust's success
>   the £5 vouchers
>   the High Street chemists
>
>   the chief executive
>   the NHS
>   the staff union
>
> b a top manager's pay
>   a £5 Boots voucher
>   a reward

Extension activities
- Students can collect similar short texts that they have exploited for particular grammatical structures. These can then be exchanged within the group.
- Students can design some questions to accompany the text to test their partner's language awareness.
- Students can also be encouraged to bring similar texts into class for group language awareness-raising activities.

Keeping a record of your learning

We have found it a fascinating exercise to see the various ways in which students reflect on what they have learned (ranging from those learners who seem to do nothing between one lesson and the next through to those who very diligently record every new vocabulary item they come across). We recognise that all learners are different and have preferred styles of learning. The Review page is designed to encourage students to reflect on what has been learned (always remembering that this isn't necessarily what you have taught!), to record vocabulary for later revision, to give opinions on particular activities, etc. The Student's Book provides an example of how the Review page was filled in by one of our students; this is intended purely as an example and is not meant to be prescriptive. You may find it useful to check periodically that the Review page is being used.

2 Education

PART ONE
Gender in education (SB page 17)

Lead-in

There are no set answers to these questions and the listening activity will be spoilt if 'answers' are given at this stage. However, the following questions could be useful in prompting students.

a:
Can they think of any reasons why girls should be addressed differently from boys?

b, c, d, e:
These questions examine the duties allocated to boys and girls at school. List the duties students had at school. Logically boys might be asked to move heavy objects but who might be given responsible jobs or asked to 'tidy up'? Obviously gender stereotypes would have a part to play here.

f, g:
Are girls treated with more respect than boys? Why might a teacher feel justified in ordering a boy to do something, yet choose to ask a girl?

h, i:
If, as educationalists believe, boys are given far more attention in class than girls, why might this be so? Do boys and girls act in ways that might lead to them gaining unequal attention time? Who usually does the most talking? Who might the teacher be more aware of in the class, boys or girls?

Listening technique

1
Answers

According to Janice Winterbottom, the questions above relate to boys and girls as follows:

Girls: b, c, e, f
Boys: a, d, g, h, i

2 Students listen a second time and complete the chart with as much information as possible. They should be encouraged to share information and maybe listen a third time if necessary before reporting back to the class.

Answers

Use of names: Through the use of family names for boys and first names for girls, boys are seen as deserving less respect than girls.

Tidying jobs: Giving girls tidying jobs, tasks they are seen as 'good at', means that stereotyped images are confirmed.

Heavy duty jobs: These are given to boys, which reinforces the idea that boys are strong and girls are weak.

Responsible jobs: These are given to girls, which implies boys can't be trusted, and maybe that girls are there to serve others.

Contributions and attention time: Boys talk for 75% of the time, girls for 25%. The result of this is that boys tend to get more attention from the teacher in similar proportions. This can lead to girls being reluctant to offer their opinions whilst boys feel their contributions are more valid.

3 After completing the listening exercise, students should be encouraged to give their own opinions on this issue. In a mixed-sex group, discussion could start by analysing who has been doing the most speaking in the group, male or female students. However, at such an early stage in the course this might prove difficult. Students' experience, both within education and in society generally, might prove more fruitful. Students from certain cultural backgrounds might find these gender roles justified, in which case discussion could centre around an informal presentation of the roles/duties of boys and girls in their culture.

Reading technique: predicting

This text, taken from *The Guardian*, examines the unequal distribution of degree awards in British universities.

Pre-reading activity
Give the students the following questions before reading.

a What's a 'Degree'?
b What's a 'First', 'Second' and a 'Third'?
c What do the following stand for: B.A., M.A., B.Sc., M.Sc., Ph.D.?

d What's the difference between a 'tutorial' and a 'seminar'?

e If your results were based partly on 'continuous assessment', what would this mean?

Answers

a An academic title given by a university or college.

b These are different classes of Degree, a First being the highest.

c B.A. Bachelor of Arts
M.A. Master of Arts
B.Sc. Bachelor of Science
M.Sc. Master of Science
Ph.D. Doctor of Philosophy

d Both a tutorial and a seminar are periods of instruction at a university or college. A tutorial is usually smaller, often consisting of only one or two students.

e Continuous assessment means assessing the student's progress over the course of a year or a term, rather than on the basis of examinations alone.

Students can explain how the above points relate to the university system in their own country, if this is known.

Students read the introduction to the article and discuss their ideas as a class. They should be encouraged to discuss whether or not any of the factors in the previous listening activity could lead to unequal results being awarded.

Reading technique: skimming

Insist that students try to complete the reading in the time allowed (two minutes). They could be encouraged to read the opening sentences to each paragraph or to search the text for paragraphs that seem to offer the most relevant material. It is very important that students get into the habit of reading quickly, and in order to assess their progress in this area they can be asked to record how far into the text they were when the two minutes were up. They should keep a record of this on the Review page for future reference when they next do a similar exercise, to see if they have improved.

Reading technique: specific information

1 This activity practises question forms and comprehension, the first pair to finish being the winners. The winning pair's questions can be written on the board and other pairs comment on the grammar/appropriateness of each. Points can be awarded for suitable corrections.

Answers

In terms of sentence structure, the following are only sample answers and several alternatives are possible.

a How many more men get Firsts compared to women?

b How many people think that this is because women are more stupid than men?

c On what kind of courses do women get equal proportions of Firsts?

d When might a woman perform less well in an examination?

e How do some women feel about tutorials?

f When are girls often praised?

g Why do men get more Firsts and Thirds?

h Why are women less keen on taking risks?

i How many people attended the seminar on women's art?

j Are men more likely to vocalise their opinions?

In pairs, students can write their own statements based on other areas of the text and give them to another pair to form the questions.

2 This activity brings to an end the issue of gender and education and students should be given the opportunity to express their own views on the subject. Point out that these issues are taken very seriously by many educationalists and sociologists. To what extent do the students feel that they reflect their own experiences?

See Language awareness: questions (1) (page 11)

Vocabulary development: common expressions

1 Students change the sentence extract using an 'as ... as' construction.

Answer

Men aren't as stupid as women.

Students find at least five examples in the text that could be expressed with 'as ... as' constructions, then rewrite them using this structure.

Answers

• Women get as many Firsts as men.
• Women can't argue as well as men in academic situations.
• Girls aren't expected to be as diverse as boys.
• Women students aren't as keen on taking risks as men.

- Women aren't as willing as men to venture views that can be totally ridiculous.
- Women don't make as many interruptions as men.

2 This exercise introduces students to some common English idioms which feature the 'as ... as' construction. Students should first try to complete the expressions that have an obvious link.

Possible answers

- as cold as ice
- as light as a feather
- as flat as a pancake
- as quiet as a mouse

3 Students then link any that have the same first letter.

Answers

- as cool as a cucumber
- as fit as a fiddle
- as pretty as a picture
- as dead as a doornail
- as good as gold
- as large as life

Students will then be in a position to make calculated guesses as to the remaining links.

Answers

- as smooth as a baby's bottom
- as dry as a bone
- as regular as clockwork
- as good as new
- as old as the hills

4 Finally, they check their answers in a dictionary and note which of these idioms are used to describe animate objects (A), inanimate objects (I), or both (B).

Answers

A as quiet as a mouse
   as cool as a cucumber
   as fit as a fiddle
   as good as gold

I as flat as a pancake
   as good as new

B as cold as ice
   as smooth as a baby's bottom
   as dry as a bone
   as light as a feather
   as pretty as a picture
   as regular as clockwork
   as old as the hills
   as large as life
   as dead as a doornail

Extension activity

This will offer an ideal opportunity for students to practise weak forms with the schwa sound /ə/ in 'as ... as'. This can be practised in isolation first, with students then being asked to write sentences incorporating several of these idioms. Correct sentences could be awarded points, the class acting as judges with you as adjudicator.

PART TWO
Education East and West (SB page 20)

The listening activity and the Exam Focus text both examine the issue of educational systems, in particular that in Japan compared to the West. The topic may be of intrinsic interest to some students but will doubtless prove far more fruitful if students are allowed to express personal opinions based on their own experiences of education.

Lead-in

1–2 The statements in this lead-in activity are aimed at generating opinions on some fundamental educational principles which, in one form or another, the students will have had first-hand experience of. Encourage them to give reasons for their choices rather than simply choosing a or b.

Listening technique

1 Students listen to the interview for the first time and decide whether Susan's opinions agree with their own. Weaker students can be asked in terms of general agreement or disagreement, stronger students might want to respond with more specific details.

2 Students decide whether the statements a–h are true or false.

Answers

a	false
b	true
c	true
d	true
e	true
f	false
g	true
h	false

3 Students should be allowed to offer opinions on what they have listened to but should save any lengthy discussion until after the Exam Focus activity which offers another insight into the Japanese system.

EXAM FOCUS: (English in Use, Section C) discourse cloze

This is the first Exam Focus in the Student's Book and possibly the first time most of the students have attempted a CAE type exercise. Remind them of the format of the English in Use paper and explain the principles behind the discourse cloze.

It is extremely important that students are encouraged at this early stage to see the Exam Focus activities as training opportunities rather than simply a form of testing. In view of this, they should be encouraged either to work co-operatively during the exercise or to compare their answers when they have finished, and you should withhold correct answers until discussion has been exhausted. Insist that students read the instructions following the Exam Focus before attempting the exercise, as these give some useful tips on how to approach the activity.

1 Give students a few minutes to read through the text to get a general understanding and to choose from extracts A–J to complete as much of the text as they feel able to. Allow students to compare their answers before moving on to Activity 2.

2 Students should now concentrate on checking their answers in terms of grammatical form. The text contains several clues to the correct choice of extract which they should be encouraged to find. For example, extract F ends with the word 'objection', normally followed by 'to'. After 'university' in extract D one would expect to find a pronoun or a noun, not a verb. Encourage students to justify some of their choices in similar ways before giving them the answers.

Answers

0	I	4	F
1	D	5	C
2	G	6	J
3	A		

See **Language awareness: dependent prepositions (page 11)**

Writing skill: a letter to a newspaper

This activity offers students the opportunity to practise formal letter writing in the form of a letter to a newspaper. It would be very useful if they could be shown some real examples of this kind of writing from British national newspapers like *The Times*, *The Guardian*, *The Independent*, etc. before attempting the activity themselves.

1 Students read the letter and decide if their response is going to agree or disagree with the sentiments expressed. It will be helpful at this stage if students with the same opinions could be paired up, as this will avoid confusion during the initial drafting stage.

2 Students work in pairs and organise their points using the model in the Students' Book. At this stage encourage them to write notes rather than trying to write the finished letter, which could be completed for homework.

PART THREE
Teacher, you're the tops (SB page 23)

Lead-in

Students express their views on what makes a good teacher. To get the ball rolling, they can be asked to think of some pleasant and not so pleasant memories of teachers at junior or high school: they could think of their best and worst memory and then report back in small groups. Students should then match the nine statements in the lead-in with the descriptions a–i.

Answers

- 'He used to treat us all in the same way' – fair-minded
- 'Our teacher was always telling funny stories' – a good sense of humour
- 'I used to have a crush on one of my teachers' – attractive looks/personality
- 'She was really tough on us' – a strict disciplinarian

- 'She never minded explaining things over and over again' – patient
- 'My teacher was a real expert in her field' – well-informed/up-to-date
- 'He really loved his subject' – enthusiastic/ stimulating
- 'If we ever had any personal problems' – good counsellor
- 'We had to work hard in class' – demanding

Vocabulary development: the language of discussing

1 In pairs brainstorm phrases for agreeing and dis-agreeing.

2 Students put each of the phrases into the correct category.

Answers

Introducing or adding points
Another thing is ...
My feeling is that ...
From my point of view ...
Personally speaking ...

Agreeing
Sure
Exactly!

Partly agreeing
I suppose that's true ...
That's true to a certain extent/degree

Politely disagreeing
Well, yes but ...
I'm not sure I agree with you on that
My feeling is that ... (stress on 'my')
From my point of view ... (stress on 'my')
Personally speaking ... (stress on 'personally')

Asking for repetition or explanation
Pardon?
What did you say?
Sorry
What do you mean by that exactly?

EXAM FOCUS: (Speaking, Section C and D) discussion and reaching agreement

Explain the format of the Speaking paper and tell students that in Section C they will have a problem solving task to discuss. Explain that it is not necessary to find 'a solution' and that it is acceptable to

disagree with points their partner has made. Point out that this section in particular gives students the chance to show their interactive skills – students who try to take over the conversation by doing all the talking will be penalised. They should get into the habit of asking opinions and of responding to comments directly rather than trying to operate independently.

1 Allow students a few minutes to rank the qualities of a good teacher from 1 to 9 (1 = most important, 9 = least important). Encourage them to think about their own experiences as this will give them more to talk about.

2 Students should now pair up and follow the instructions in the Exam Focus, having the discussion and then commenting on how well each of them used the given expressions.

Writing skill: a report for a competition entry

1 Students read the competition details from *She* magazine. Explain that the students are to imagine they are entering the competition and to choose a teacher they admire or respect to write about.

2 Students should refer to the qualities listed in the lead-in activity for Part Three and think of particular instances where these qualities were demonstrated. If this is done in class, students could work in pairs, telling their partner about some of these memories as they make notes.

3 When students feel they have sufficient notes they should write the first draft of their report. When they have finished the pairs swap work and give their partners a grade out of 20 according to these criteria:

- **Language**: accuracy of grammar/vocabulary/ spelling – 10 points
- **Content**: interest/persuasiveness/final impression on the reader – 10 points

Most students will be quick to point out weaknesses in accuracy! However they should be encouraged to think seriously about how interesting or persuasive they found the report and for what reasons. They should try to put themselves in the position of the magazine editor and try to decide if the report would have a favourable effect on him/her. This has as much to do with style as it does with accuracy! Having made comments on each other's work and with some feedback from you, the students should be in a position to write a final draft for homework. There is a sample student answer on page 150 of the Student's Book.

Extension activity
When the final drafts have all been completed, the reports can be pinned around the classroom to be judged by the class. Each student can give each report marks based on the grades in Activity 3 above. The marks can then be collected and collated, the student with the highest mark being the winner. A selection of some of the best reports can be photocopied and given to the students to use for future reference.

LANGUAGE AWARENESS: dependent prepositions

1 Students supply the correct preposition in each sentence. Encourage them to experiment with the different sounds when each preposition is tried. Quite often, the correct choice is the one that sounds the best. When they have finished, students check their answers from the text.

Answers
a dependent on
b proportions of
c suffer from
d praised for
e keen on
f lose confidence in
g compared to/with
h mirrored by aversion to
i the inequalities inherent in

2 Students match the appropriate prepositions with the phrases.

Answers
a for a start
b on balance
c by any chance
d at long last
e in any case
f in other words
g from time to time
h on the whole
i on purpose
j by mistake
k at least
l in addition to
m on average
n with respect to
o from now on
p for a change

q at all costs
r by all means
s in confidence
t on no account
u in a hurry
v on the surface

3 This exercise gives students the chance to check that they understand the meaning of some of these expressions.

Answers
a on purpose
b for a change
c in confidence
d in a hurry
e by any chance
f with respect to
g by all means
h on the whole
i from now on/for a change
j from time to time

Refer students to the Exam Tip which points out the importance of dependent prepositions in the English in Use paper. Encourage students to keep a record of these.

Extension activity
Students can write dialogues expressing the meanings of those expressions that remain.

LANGUAGE AWARENESS: questions (1)

The first section deals with two structures that enable people involved in a conversation to interact with each other: reply questions and 'helpers' such as 'really?', 'seriously?', etc.

1 Ask students if, in their culture, women are often seen as 'gossips' – if, compared to men, women are supposed to speak much more in informal conversations. If this is so in their culture, ask them if they have any ideas why it might be so. Students listen to the short conversation between a husband and his wife as an example of how not to participate in a conversation.

2 Students listen again and comment on the kind of words or phrases the husband could have used to show he is interested, surprised etc. and which would make the conversation more interactive. If students aren't sure, avoid giving them 'answers' at this stage.

3 Students now listen to a second conversation between two women. Students make notes of the words and phrases used that show interest, surprise, agreement, etc.

Answers

Really? (helper)
You're joking? (helper)
Has she? (reply question)
Did they? (reply question)
Did she? (reply question)
Seriously? (helper)
Is that right? (helper)
Didn't they? (reply question)
weren't they? (reply question)

4 Reply questions that mean 'I agree' are always negative. Otherwise, reply questions usually follow the (+) (+) or (−) (−) model: that is, a positive question replies to a positive statement and a negative question to a negative statement. If students have difficulty choosing the correct verb in the reply question, refer them to the Language Awareness sections covering both reply questions and question tags.

E.g. 'It was a lovely film.' 'Yes wasn't it?'
'I've just come back from Japan'. 'Have you?'
'We went to Spain last year.' 'Did you?'

5 Students supply the correct reply question for each of the statements.

Answers

a I've just seen a great film. Have you?
b I had to go to the doctor's yesterday. Did you?
c Julia's really grown. Yes, hasn't she?
d I'd love to be rich. Would you?
e I'd never been abroad before my last holiday. Hadn't you?
f He has his haircut every week. Does he?
g They had a beautiful house in the country. Did they?
h What a terrible film that was. Yes. Wasn't it?
i I'd prefer to leave early. Would you?
j Nothing scares me. Doesn't it?
k I'll be on holiday this time next week. Will you?

6 Students listen to a recording of the 'Yes–No' game. The rules to this are very simple: the person playing the game must try to last one minute without saying either 'yes' or 'no'. As students listen to the recording they should note the way the interviewer uses 'helpers' and reply questions to catch the contestant out.

7 Depending on the size of the class, this activity can either be carried out as a whole class activity or in smaller groups. Ask for volunteers – anybody who feels they can last the minute. Monitor the questions asked and make a note of any mistakes made with questions. These can be written up on the board afterwards for feedback.

8 This activity tries to raise awareness of the various functions that questions can have and how misunderstandings can occur. In pairs or groups, students look at the short dialogues and explain the cause of the misunderstandings.

Answers

a 'Excuse me?' functions here as 'Can you help me?', not 'Sorry' as B seems to think.
b 'How do you do?' functions as a greeting, not a question. The response is often simply 'How do you do?'

a 'What do you do?' means 'What is your job?'. B interprets it as meaning 'What do you do at a specific (unspecified) time?'
b 'How are you?' is a question and means 'Is everything OK?' B interprets it wrongly as a greeting on the lines of 'How do you do?'.

a 'Can you open the window?' is a request. B interprets it (deliberately and jokingly) as a question of ability.
b 'What's she like?' means 'Describe her looks and personality', not 'What does she like doing?'

a 'Have you got the time?' is a request. B (deliberately and jokingly) interprets it as a question.
b 'How long will the car be in the garage?' refers to time. B (deliberately and jokingly) interprets it as referring to length.

Refer students to the Exam Tip and encourage them to practise their interactive skills in future conversations.

Citizens of the World

PART ONE
Missing home? (SB page 28)

Lead-in

Students work together to discuss how much they know about life in Britain as a lead-in to the listening in which young foreign adults give their insights into the British way of life. Ask each group to report to the whole class on two or three of the topics given.

Further discussion points

Is there a difference between popular stereotypes of their own nationalities (or of neighbouring countries) and the reality?

Listening technique: global understanding

1 For those students who have already been to Britain, would they consider going again? What did they most like and dislike about British life?

2 Students listen and identify which topics each speaker mentions. This is purely for global understanding.

Answers

Gusta – food
Petros – studying in Britain, attitudes to foreigners
Andrea – family life, living standards

Listening technique: specific information

Play the tape again for students to attempt these true/false questions. Statements a and b for each speaker are concerned with content; statement c is to test inference about the attitude of the speaker. After listening, students can share answers in pairs. As the extracts are short, they can listen again if necessary.

Answers

Gusta		Petros		Andrea	
a	F	a	F	a	F
b	T	b	F	b	T
c	T	c	T	c	T

Speaking skill: making and dealing with interruptions

Students at lower levels often lack the skills to converse in English in a natural-sounding way. This is a light-hearted activity which gives the students a chance to mimic native speaker conversations. As an alternative, you could put students into groups of three, with one student monitoring which of the phrases are used correctly, or which other phrases not listed are used.

Vocabulary development: getting around

1 This is a challenging exercise designed to help students understand the various shades of meaning for these ways of travelling/getting around. We suggest that students use a good monolingual dictionary for this exercise. Failing that, you could give them the following list of dictionary definitions.

- to go globetrotting – (informal) to travel through many countries seeing as many different things as possible
- to live out of a suitcase – to travel so frequently that one never has time to unpack
- to nip round – (colloqiual) to pay someone (usually nearby) a short visit
- to go for a spin – (informal)to take a short ride for pleasure, usually by car or bike
- to see the world – to travel world-wide
- to go back-packing – a low-cost way of travelling in which one's luggage is carried on one's back in a rucksack
- to make a move – (colloquial) to begin one's return home, usually from a friend's house
- to go on an outing – to go on a short pleasure trip or excursion, usually for a day
- to bum around – (slang) to travel around aimlessly, usually on a low budget
- to get under way – similar to 'make a move'
- to be always on the move – to be travelling constantly
- to set off – (multi-word verb) to start a journey
- to pop round – (colloquial) similar to 'nip round'; to pay a visit to someone who lives nearby, e.g. a neighbour

Answers

	Long Distance	Short Distance	Departing	Budget Travel	Regular Travel
to go globetrotting	✓	☐	☐	☐	☐
to live out of a suitcase	☐	☐	☐	☐	✓
to nip round	☐	✓	☐	☐	☐
to go for a spin	☐	✓	☐	☐	☐
to see the world	✓	☐	☐	☐	☐
to go back-packing	☐	☐	☐	✓	☐
to make a move	☐	☐	✓	☐	☐
to go on an outing	☐	✓	☐	☐	☐
to bum around	☐	☐	☐	✓	☐
to get under way	☐	☐	✓	☐	☐
to be always on the move	☐	☐	☐	☐	✓
to set off	☐	☐	✓	☐	☐
to pop round	☐	✓	☐	☐	☐

2 Students use one of the expressions in each gap. Remind them to use the appropriate tense.

Answers

a make a move/get under way
b setting off
c pop round/nip round
d go for a spin
e on an outing
f went globetrotting/was always on the move

Students can record any of these expression in the Review page. Encourage them to write their own sample sentences which you can check.

EXAM FOCUS: (Writing Section B) a travel guide for your country

Although this is an Exam Focus question, there is still a lot of attention given to the process of writing here.

1 Brainstorm with the students what they think are the most important factors which make a good travel guide. Ask them to select and justify their choice for the top five criteria from the list.

2–3 Students begin the planning stages by selecting three main areas to focus on. Then encourage them to make a plan similar to the one shown. Emphasise that their advice must be tailored to their audience. Students from the same areas might benefit from discussing their ideas in small groups, but otherwise, students will probably prefer to work individually.

Before completing final drafts, they might like to look through the Language Awareness on the language of obligation which provides some useful structures for this kind of writing.

When final drafts have been completed (for homework) let students exchange essays and ask them to focus on how well the target audience has been addressed. See Writing Skills Development in the Students' Book for a sample answer and marking guidelines.

See **Language awareness: the language of obligation (page 17)**

PART TWO
Getting away (SB page 31)

Lead-in

1 Students are introduced to the topic of getting away from it all through a general knowledge quiz about famous explorers. This should be treated as a light-hearted activity with students pooling their knowledge in small groups. Allow about 10 minutes for this before checking answers.

Answers

Willem Barents	Greenland	1597
James Cook	Australia	1770
Jaques Cartier	Newfoundland	1534
Marco Polo	China	1271
Christopher Columbus	America	1492
Robert Peary	North Pole	1809
Samuel de Champlain	Quebec	1603

2 Students discuss why people like these set out on these journeys. Inquisitiveness? Financial gain? Boredom? Running away from problems at home?

Discussion points

Students discuss the issue of colonialism. How many of the countries listed above were truly 'discovered'? Which countries and their indigenous peoples were simply exploited for financial gain?

EXAM FOCUS: (Listening, Section C) mutiple choice

1 Remind students that with any listening exercise they can anticipate much of the information they are about to hear simply by reading through the questions first.

2 Students listen to the tape twice. Good students will manage with just one hearing, but weaker students will need more help. Ask weaker students to focus on the obviously incorrect answer during the first listen.

Answers

Incorrect statements:
1 A
2 A
3 A
4 D
5 B

3 Students listen for the second time and try to identify the correct answer this time from the three remaining choices.

Answers

1 C
2 C
3 *C* B
4 B
5 C

See **Language awareness: reported speech (page 18)**

Reading technique: prediction

Students quickly read the first paragraph of the extract and speculate on Paul Theroux's reasons for setting off on this journey.

Suggested answer

To get away from the unhappiness caused by the breakdown of his marriage.

Reading technique: scanning and information transfer

1 Students scan the text first (without reading for understanding) in order to find the 20 place names. Setting a time limit adds a competitive element, as does having teams working against each other.

Answers

Melanesia	San Francisco	Tora-Tora
Black Islands	Honololu	Fuji
Boston	Easter Island	Fiji
Melbourne	Polynesia	Haiti
New Zealand	California	Tahiti
Australia	Bora-Bora	Johnston
Chicago	Moora-Moora	Island

2–3
Answers

1 Boston (his birth-place), 2 London, 3 Boston, 4 Chicago, 5 San Francisco, 6 Honolulu

Reading technique: inference and speculation

Students read the text again in more detail in order to answer these questions. No answers are given here as the task is meant to be very open-ended. Allow students time to share their answers with each other.

Extension activity

1 Ask your students the following question: When reading texts in English, do you reach for your dictionary immediately if you don't know a word?

2 Students then underline all the unfamiliar words or phrases from the text, and categorise them under the following headings:

I can confidently guess the meaning of the word

I can understand the sentence even though I don't know the meaning of the word

I can't understand the sentence because I don't know the meaning of the word

3 Get students to compare their charts with their colleague's. Can they help each other to work out the meanings of the problematic words? Encourage them to use their dictionaries to check the meanings of the words under the third heading.

4 Ask students which words from the text they would want to remember:
a if they were studying medicine
b if they wanted to write a novel in English.

5 Finally, let them decide which words are important to them. And elicit the importance of learning vocabulary not just for the sake of it but because it will be useful.

PART THREE
Activity holidays (SB page 34)

Lead-in

Students allocate what they think is the most suitable (and maybe least suitable) holiday for each member of their group. Encourage them to give reasons for their choices. Obviously, students should work with people they know quite well.

Reading technique: predicting

Students read the introduction to the activity holiday article and try to guess what type of activities are available.

Answer

Working and activity holidays

EXAM FOCUS: (Reading) multiple matching

This is the first example in the book of the multiple matching question. (See also Unit 11, Part 3.) In this type of question, candidates have either a collection of short texts or a complete text with clearly labelled sections. Candidates are asked to match a list of points to the relevant text/section. This can be designed to test either scanning or skimming skills. Before students attempt the question, point them towards the rubric which follows the text.

This activity can be done under exam conditions (allow 15–20 minutes), but encourage students to share answers with each other before whole class checking. For questions 1–10, which test scanning

skills, they should underline the evidence in the text. Questions 11–15 test global understanding of each text (students have to choose the best title).

Answers

1	A	9	D
2	E	10	A, C
3	C	11	B
4	B	12	E
5	C, D	13	A
6	B, C	14	C
7	C	15	F
8	B		

Writing skills: a formal letter and an informal note

Although not labelled as an Exam Focus section, this activity replicates the type of question found on Section A of Paper 2 (Writing), in which candidates have to write a response to various types of input. Hence, reading skills and the ability to extract relevant information before writing their response are crucial. As in all writing tasks, the ability to use the appropriate level of formality is also important.

1 Students imagine they work for a travel agency and have to recommend a suitable holiday for two people. They write a formal letter to one of those (John Williams) and an informal note to a colleague advising about a suitable holiday for the other (Sally Cartwright). The inputs are:

- the articles from the previous activity on working holidays (page 35)
- a note from the secretary, Jan
- a brochure, 'Working Holidays Organisations'

2 First, let the students decide which holiday(s) they would recommend for John and Sally.

Suggested answers

John   Working Weekends on Organic Farms
Sally   Earthwatch or Discover the World

3 Students go back to the original article and underline any appropriate information from each section.

4 Elicit from students the fact that the letter should be of the relatively formal business type.

5 A suitable framework for the letter might be:

Dear Mr Williams,
     Thank you for your enquiry of (date) regarding holidays for you and your family. I think the following may be of interest to you.

....
....
....
....

     If this sounds suitable, please telephone to confirm and we can proceed with the booking. Once again, thank you for your interest, and I hope to hear from you soon.

Yours sincerely
(signature)
(name)

Students then write the note to their colleague, which should be shorter and in a more informal style:

Hi Jan, thanks for the note. I've gone through our current brochure and I think Sally Cartwright's best bet would be either .... or .... Both of these ...., but she might prefer .... as ....

Extension activity

Students can be asked to proofread each other's writing for grammatical mistakes during a later lesson. Alternatively, the teacher can mark the writing and make a note of some of the mistakes made. A 'sentence auction' could then be offered during the following lesson which is run on the following lines.

The teacher writes up on the board a selection of correct and incorrect sentences found in the students' writing. Students are then told they have an amount of money (£100 is a nice round figure). Explain that they are at an auction and that their aim is to buy as many correct sentences as possible but not to waste their money on incorrect sentences. Start the auction and ask for bids on one sentence before moving on to the next. If students try to correct the sentence before it has been sold, tell them to be quiet as they will have a chance to comment on the accuracy of the sentence after it has been sold – if it is sold! Remind students that they can only spend £100; once this has been used up they can no longer participate in the auction.

LANGUAGE AWARENESS: the language of obligation

1 Students read through the list of words and phrases and decide which are generally used in formal and informal situations. Remind students to keep a record of these structures on the formal/ informal Record Sheet on page 147.

Answers

Formal	you are obliged to
	it is advisable
	to be permitted
	you are required
	you are recommended
	it is not necessary to
	it is the reponsibility of
Informal	it's best if
	mustn't (contraction)
	needn't (contraction)
	don't need to (contraction)
Both	must
	ought to
	have to
	should
	you should avoid
	to be allowed to

2 Students listen to the dialogue, and if need be turn to the tapescript on page 156. They listen for or underline in the tapescript all the examples of informal words or phrases expressing obligation. The answers below include all the phrases of obligation in the dialogue, some of which appear in the 'Both' category above.

Answers

it's best if
should
don't need to
not allowed to
don't have to
ought to
have to
mustn't
needn't

3 This activity approximates to the 'Sentences from notes' activity in the English in Use paper. Students write out the sentences in full, replacing the informal words or phrases highlighted with their formal equivalents. The word order will occasionally need to be changed.

Suggested answers

- Visas are not required for visits of less than one month.
- Although not required, cholera and typhoid vaccinations are recommended.
- It is the responsibility of the individual not to exceed the duty-free allowance.
- Tourists are not permitted to take photographs in restricted areas.
- It is advisable to seek local information regarding nude sunbathing.
- Tourists are required to obtain adequate health insurance for health care.
- It is advisable to hire a car before arriving

4 Students compare the pairs of sentences for different meanings. Allow them to do this first without your help. They can then check their ideas in the Grammar Reference section.

Answers

a They didn't reserve a seat because they knew it wouldn't be necessary.
b They reserved a seat but then realised it hadn't been necessary.

a Stated with authority. The statement would have been written or spoken by an airport official.
b Referring to obligations that do not emanate from the authority of the speaker. Possibly stated by a friend who is simply stating what the airport authorities demand.

a An explanation of when the person should arrive at the airport (in the future).
b The person is late (highlighting the past modal form and its meaning).

a On one occasion.
b Generally the case (highlighting the fact that 'could' cannot be used to refer to permission on one occasion).

5 Students complete the sentences with the appropriate verb. Remind them of the importance of using the correct form.

Answers

a It's been sunny since we left the house. We needn't have brought this umbrella.
b We didn't need to telephone. We knew they were expecting us.
c You should have ordered ordered the tickets sooner. We'll never get a seat now.
d Don't miss the next train or you'll have to walk home.
e You know the rules, son. You must tell us if you're coming home late.
f My parents were quite easy going. But I had to do my fair share of housework.
g I'll always the remember the first time I was allowed to smoke at home. It was a really strange feeling.
h Excuse me. Can I open this window?

Exam tip
Point out to students that these formal and informal structures will be useful in Paper 2 (Writing) and Paper 3 (English in Use), Section B.

LANGUAGE AWARENESS: reported speech

1 This activity is aimed at raising awareness of the major patterns in reported speech. Students read the seven statements and match them with the correct grammatical forms.

Answers

The book advised her not to drink the tap water. (g)

The agent told him he should arrive at the airport two hours early. (b)

The travel guide pointed out that travellers cheques were difficult to change. (c)

The hotel manager agreed to offer him a different room. (f)

The passenger admitted flying scared her to death. (a)

Her friend congratulated her on choosing such a nice hotel. (d)

He boasted about getting the highest marks. (e)

2 Students decide in which category each of the verbs can be placed. Remind them that some verbs can be used in more than one category. Some less common patterns have been omitted.

Answers

a suggest
  deny

b assure
  promise
  remind

c threaten
  promise
  explain
  suggest
  deny
  agree
  accept

d threaten
  accuse
  remind
  invite

e apologise (for)
  agree (with/about/on)

f threaten
  promise
  agree
  offer

g invite
  encourage
  beg
  remind

3 Students convert the direct speech into reported speech. This activity is restricted to sentence level conversion to give students confidence in using the verb patterns correctly (Activity 4 gives them the chance to report statements more authentically). Remind students to report the statements from the point of view of the arresting officer. Draw their attention to the change in time referencing in reported speech (see italicised text in the answers).

Suggested answers

He threatened to get his big brother if I *kept* bothering him.
He denied being anywhere near the bank *that* morning.
He accused me of planting the money on him.
He offered to buy me a drink.

He agreed that he *looked* suspicious with the mask he *had* on.
He accepted that he *didn't have* a leg to stand on.
He begged me not to arrest him ... his wife *would* kill him.
He promised he *would* be a good boy if I let him go.
He suggested that we split the money 50–50.

4–5 Students listen to and read the answerphone messages and then convert them into written reports. Students match suitable verbs to the numbers in the messages. Point out that if the report is to look authentic, they should not report every word, but merely the essence of the messages.

Suggested answers

Mr Laurent phoned from Paris. He explained that he still hadn't received his tickets and accused us of not bothering about his earlier complaint. He reminded us of the business we receive from his company and threatened to take his custom elsewhere unless he received his tickets. He suggested that we phone him immediately.

We phoned him back and left a message. We assured him that the tickets would be ready to collect from the airport but also offered to deliver them to his office. We apologised for inconveniencing him and admitted that we had been rather slow in delivering them. Finally, we encouraged him to continue dealing with us.

Extension activity

Ask for a volunteer from the group (somebody who is very quick-witted) to play the role of a fortune-teller. This person should leave the room. Students then go out to speak to the fortune-teller individually and will be given three pieces of information: something about their past, their present and their future. As one student returns, another should be sent out. Each returning student should tell the class the three pieces of information they were given, using reported speech of course.

E.g. She claimed I'd had lots of arguments with my sister as a child.
She said I was working rather hard at the moment.
She promised that I would come into a lot of money in the near future.

UNIT 4

Health Issues

PART ONE
Alternative medicine (SB page 40)

Lead-in

Students identify the examples of alternative medicine shown in the pictures, which are massage, acupuncture, reflexology, aromatherapy, herbal medicine. Hold a brief discussion on the different types of alternative medicine, to give students the chance to air their own knowledge of the subject and to raise anticipation for the reading and listening activities. You could develop the question of whether these methods can/should replace traditional Western treatments.

Reading technique: predicting

Students read the introduction to the article 'Acupuncture gets to the point' and the teacher quickly elicits some reactions to the paragraph. Would anybody be willing to try it?

EXAM FOCUS: (Reading) sentence and paragraph cloze

This activity replicates one of the questions in Paper 1 in which candidates must read a text which has several sentences or paragraphs removed and recreate the text by selecting from a number of options. The aim is to test students' knowledge of cohesion and organisation of the text. There is usually at least one distractor.

1–2 Encourage students to try the activity first and then to reflect on the strategies that they used to choose their answers. We have found with this kind of activity that it is useful to get students to justify their choices to each other, even (indeed especially) if they have differing answers. You will find a similar activity in Unit 12, in which students are given tips for completing this kind of exercise.

Answers

a 8	c 3	e 6	g 5
b 1	d 2	f 4	

Listening technique: global understanding

Students listen to the text and check their global understanding by ordering the topics correctly. As the tape is quite lengthy, encourage students to complete the task after the first listening only.

Answers

1 c
2 e
3 a
4 f
5 d
6 b

Listening technique: specific information

Students listen and decide how many factual mistakes there are in the letter. Ask them to check their answers in pairs or small groups.

Answers

- confidence
- Alternative medicine can have side effects
- basically makes you feel full of energy
- I have received treatment myself in China
- It was during my stay in China that I started my training
- One aspect of the course examined whether acupuncture can treat people of different sizes and shapes
- In the future I hope to train in homeopathy and aromatherapy
- a rural clinic would allow me to be free from the stresses of modern life

Extension activity

Students listen to the interview a third time and correct the mistakes that were made. They can then rewrite the letter to the organisation, using appropriate formal letter writing conventions.

Vocabulary development: some common expressions

1–2 Students can work in pairs or small groups for this. Encourage them to compare the expressions with those in their own language, sharing any interesting features with the whole class. They should write their own explanation (in English) for each of the expressions (a–h).

Answers

a sick
b sickness
c ill
d ill
e healthy
f sick
g health
h sick

See **Language awareness: defining and non-defining relative clauses (page 24)**

PART TWO
Smoking (SB page 43)

Lead-in

Begin by getting students to read the statements on smoking and to discuss their views. Hold a feedback session and develop the discussion with questions such as:

- Who in the class smokes?
- Who has recently given up?
- What drives people to want to start smoking?
- Where should people be allowed to/prohibited from smoking?

Reading technique: predicting

1–2 Students read through the list of vocabulary and try to predict the content of the article on smoking. They should then skim the text as quickly as possible to see if their predictions were correct (if one minute is too short, negotiate a reasonable time with the class). Encourage students to time themselves, reminding them that the CAE exam requires speedy and efficient reading in Paper 1 and Paper 2 Section A.

Reading technique: summary skills

1 Students work together to match the headings A–F with the appropriate paragraphs. Don't worry if there is some disagreement over this: the students can work profitably in pairs trying to justify their choices. A useful method is to ask them to underline evidence in their chosen paragraph.

Answers

A 1 ('improve ... at a stroke'; 'dramatic and almost immediate improvement')
B 4 ('expert opinions were sharply polarised')
C 11
D 8 ('a very good investment')
E 6 ('A word is deeply relevant to the problem')
F 10

2 Students write their own headings for paragraphs 2, 3, 5, 7 and 9. As an optional activity, they can test them out on their partner.

Reading technique: comprehension

1–3 Students can gain an insight into the design of multiple choice questions by trying to write such questions themselves. This activity may take quite a while so you can set it for homework if time is short. When the questions have been completed, one group should test the other. Students can put the questions onto an overhead transparency, or you can photocopy them.

Suggested rules

- Each group asks their questions in turn. (The class should decide whether or not the texts can be referred to by the group answering the questions.)
- Each question correctly answered gains two points.
- Between one and three points can be awarded to the opposing group for gramatically incorrect questions.
- You should intervene only when no agreement can be reached.

See **Language awareness: passive or active? (page 24)**

Listening technique: specific information

1 Before students listen, remind them that they should read through the statements first (as with all listening tests).

Answers

a false
b true
c true
d false
e false
f false

2–3 To finish off the listening and to act as a lead-in to the writing, these questions ask students to respond to what they have read and heard so far about smoking. This is a useful point at which to see if any of the anti-smokers have become more sympathetic to smoking.

Writing skill: a magazine article

Students have to write an article for a student magazine on how to give up smoking.

Extension activity

Group discussion on the best way to give up smoking. Students work to rank different methods in order of their effectiveness (1–6), weighing up the pros and cons for young people.

Examples:

willpower	nicotine chewing gum
nicotine patches	alternative therapies
fake cigarettes	support group

If you put these methods on the board this will provide useful additional vocabulary input for the writing task.

1   First, students need to plan the content of the article. Encourage them to use the input they have encountered so far in the unit, but in addition they can share ideas or anecdotes from their personal experiences.

2   Guide students towards the fact that, as the target audience are young students, an informal tone would be most appropriate.

3   Activity 3, although subjective, highlights the positive effects that can be created by constructing opening sentences that 'grab' the readers' attention. Students will no doubt prefer opening sentences b and c to the other two; try to get them to articulate why. Suggestions may include: use of the second person to address the reader (i.e. 'you' is more personal than 'young people'); use of shock tactics.

4   Students write a first draft in class (allow about 45 minutes for this if you can). If there is time, the students should exchange drafts and comment on the appeal of each other's articles. They should write a final draft at home.
There is a sample student answer on page 151 of the student's Book.

PART THREE
Stress and anxiety (SB page 45)

Lead-in

1–2 Students work by themselves to complete the quiz on evaluating levels of stress. Before holding the discussion see the extension activity below. If students are happy to discuss their scores with each other, they can compare lifestyles to see if there is an appreciable difference between those with low and high scores.

If they have problems with any vocabulary, encourage them to discuss possible meanings with each other. They should use their knowledge of the context to aid vocabulary guessing

E.g. 'run down' and 'tired' are probably similar in meaning.
'grip' probably means 'to hold tightly'.

Extension activity

The Student's Book tells the students to compare their scores with others. This feedback session can be extended to include a report on how well the discussions went in terms of interactive skills. To do this, a student in each group can monitor the discussion. This tends to work better if the students in discussion are unaware of the points the third student is monitoring – knowledge of this can make the conversation rather unnatural. The monitoring student can work from a checklist, making notes of each of the following:

• Who contributed most to the discussion?
• If one student was doing most of the talking, how many times did he/she ask for the opinion of other members of the group?
• If one student was very quiet, was this because other students were trying to take over the conversation?
• How many times did students use the following phrases to show they were interested? Tick each one every time you hear it.
Really?   Seriously?
Have you?   Did you?
• Did either student use any of the phrases for agreeing and disagreeing listed in the vocabulary exercise in Unit 2, Part Three?
• What was your overall opinion of the discussion?

Exploring pronunciation: word stress

Students sort out where the main word stress occurs in the list of words. They should work in pairs and be encouraged to say the words out loud. Students can check answers in a dictionary or with you.

Answers

First syllable
difficulty
vulnerable
anxious
confidence
irritated
pressure

Second syllable
frustrated (but in Am Eng the stress is usually on the first syllable)
enthusiasm
impatience
distracting

Third syllable
indecisive
overwhelmed

A useful tip for students is that in negative forms of words, for example, 'indecisive' (negative form of 'decisive') or 'impatience' ('patience') the main stress is never on the negative prefix.

Extension activity

Students find and complete word families for as many of these items as possible.

E.g. difficulty (n.) – difficult (adj.)
frustrated (adj.) – frustrate (v.)

Speaking skill: discussion and reaching agreement

1 Elict from students whether stress is treated as seriously as other illnesses in the workplace. If not, then should it be?

2–3 Point out to students that this type of activity (discussion and reaching agreement) features in Section C of Paper 5. Allow at least 15 minutes for this activity, particularly if the group contains four or more students. Ask students to report back to you at the end of the activity with their selections for the most and least stressful jobs, and with justifications for their choice.

Your students may be interested in the following stress ratings which appeared in a magazine:

secretary	4.3
bus or train driver	5.4
managing director	5.8
politician	7.0
surgeon	6.8
teacher	6.2

EXAM FOCUS: (English in Use, Section B) proofreading skills

Make sure that students read the instructions to the exercise carefully. They should note that they are required to correct spelling or punctuation errors. We have found that students doing this activity often make (unnecessary) grammatical corrections, having failed to appreciate the kind of corrections that are required. The teacher may wish to refer students to page 93 for an outline of punctuation.

Answers

1 neccessary – necessary
2 : – .
3 ✓
4 but, provided – but provided
5 stimmulated – stimulated
6 ✓
7 however – however,
8 controll – control
9 and, as – and as
10 desease – disease
11 count's – counts
12 no comma after 'problems'
13 ✓
14 innability – inability

Listening technique: note taking

1–3 Students listen to a doctor talking about the symptoms of and treatment for anxiety. This activity practises note taking skills and students should be encouraged to disregard unimportant information and to write notes and abbreviations rather than trying to write out full words and/or sentences. They should refer to the tapescript to check that they have made note of important information.

Writing skill: an advice leaflet

1–3 Students use the notes they have made from the listening activity as the basis for a leaflet giving advice on anxiety to professional people.

They can prepare the leaflet in class, deciding on the organisation and content in pairs or groups before doing the writing for homework. Ask students to discuss the appropriate tone of the leaflet, which should be sympathetic and reassuring.

LANGUAGE AWARENESS:
defining and non-defining relative clauses

1 Students try to solve the problem, which presents the difference between defining and non-defining relative clauses with the relative pronoun 'who'. The puzzle will be made easier if students not only tick the appropriate sections but also blank out the boxes that aren't used. Insist that students work collaboratively in teams. This will give you the chance to monitor their use of these structures as they share their ideas.

Answers
- Alma is the lawyer. She took up golf and pulled a muscle.
- Gail is the housewife. She took up tennis and won a silver cup.
- Ivy is the tax inspector. She took up rowing and dislocated her shoulder.
- Mary is the secretary. She took up cycling and broke her wrist.

2
Answers
- 'That' can replace 'who' in clues a, e, f and g (defining).
- The use of commas in clues b, c, d and h indicates that the information within the commas is extra, not necessary, information (non-defining).

3 Students examine the sentences and summarise the main differences between defining and non-defining relative clauses by completing the table.

Answers
- Necessary information: a, d, f
- Extra information: b, c, e
- Commas: b, c, e
- Use of 'that': a, d, f
- Omission of pronoun: a, d (not f because the relative pronoun is the subject and therefore cannot be omitted, but do not tell the students this at this stage; see Activity 4)
- Defining: a, d, f
- Non-defining: b, c, e

4 The relative pronoun can usually be omitted in defining relative clauses unless the pronoun is the subject of the clause.

5 Students re-read the article on acupuncture, underlining examples of defining and non-defining relative pronouns. Encourage them to check the uses against the rules that have been highlighted in this section.

6 Students fill in the gaps in the short text, supplying defining or non-defining relative pronouns and commas where required. Tell them to miss out the pronoun if it is possible.

Answer

Mary, who is a secretary, took up cycling. The injury (that/which) Alma sustained was caused whilst playing golf. The woman whose wrist was broken was a secretary. Mary, who took up cycling, was the woman who broke her wrist. Gail has a silver cup (that/which) she won playing tennis. Ivy's dislocated shoulder, which she got rowing a boat, is very painful. The sport (that/which) Mary hates most is golf. Gail won a trophy, which probably made the other three women rather jealous. She won the cup around the time (that/when) Ivy was nursing her dislocated shoulder.

Remind students that defining and non-defining clauses are often necessary in Paper 3 (English in Use, Section C, writing sentences from notes). Students could be given a practice test for this section to highlight the frequency of the structure in this exercise.

LANGUAGE AWARENESS:
passive or active?

1 Students re-read paragraphs 3 and 4 of 'Quit While You're Ahead' and discuss the use of the passive and active. In paragraph 3 the passive is used, as the emphasis is on the studies, not on those who carried out the studies. The active is used in paragraph 4 as the emphasis here is on the different opinions of psychologists, scientists and educators, not the studies.

2 This is another opportunity for students to find out how much they know about the use of passive and active structures. Students read the 12 sentences and decide if any of them could be improved by using active or passive constructions.

Avoid giving answers at this stage. Students should come back to this activity after they have completed Activities 3 and 4 to see if they have changed their opinions about any of the sentences.

Answers

a 58 year-old woman gives birth *has given/* (Newspaper headline. Emphasis here is on the age of the woman.)

b The coffee beans are picked and sent to the processing plant. (The description of a process. The agent is not important.)

c OK.

d If spoken, OK. If written: If your bill is not paid, further action will be taken against you.

e Unfortunately, interest rates will have to be increased next year. (Hiding responsibility.)

f The Government has reduced unemployment from 3 million to 1 million. (Taking the credit.)

g I reckon Italy will win the match.

h The thieves are believed to have escaped in a stolen car.

i This food should be consumed within 24 hours from the date of purchase. (People in general)

j OK.

k Dad? Any chance of you meeting me at the station?

l Sorry son. I can't. My car's being repaired.

3 This exercise highlights the contexts in which the passive is often used.

Answers

a In a formal letter
b A public notice
c On the packaging of perishable consumer goods
d The description of a process
e A newspaper headline

4 Students match the statements a–e with the correct use, thus summarising common uses of the passive.

Answers

a Making the statement more formal
b The agent is obvious or not known
c The agent is people in general
d When the agent is unimportant, for example when describing a process or experiment
e To shift the emphasis in a statement the agent is obvious or not known

5 Students should now be given the opportunity to check their original opinions in Activity 2. Allow them to come to any decisions themselves before giving any answers.

6 Students can work in pairs or groups and be awarded team points for every correct statement. A correct statement will consist of a statement containing a passive structure used appropriately, not one where an active construction would be preferable. Other teams should be the judge of this, with you acting as final arbiter.

Point out that active and passive structures are very useful when creating formal and informal language in Paper 2 (Writing) and Paper 3 (English in Use), Section B. Encourage students to make a note of these formal and informal structures on page 147 of the Student's Book.

UNIT 5

The World of Language

PART ONE
Foreign accent syndrome (SB page 51)

Lead-in

Try to encourage students to give specific examples of foreigners speaking in the students' native language and the typical errors they make.

E.g. 'In my language people often say X instead of Y.'
'Some people find X sound hard to pronounce.'

Reading technique: skimming

1–2 This task gives students a specific strategy for skimming a text by reading only the topic sentences in each paragraph. (Tell them that good writers often highlight the topic of each paragraph in the first sentence.) Students decide on the topic of the text by choosing from one of the alternatives a–e. If they are not sure, they can read the next sentence in the paragraph. The emphasis, however, in this activity is on reading quickly. You can add a competitive element by asking students to time themselves to see who is the first to finish.

Answer
b

2
Answer
Paragraph 2

Reading technique: finding the main ideas

1–3 Students read the text more closely to distinguish main ideas and supporting details. You might find it useful with weaker students to demonstrate the principle on the board with the following example:

'A bizarre case of language loss came to light in 1985 when a young man, then 24, had suffered a stroke.'

Ask students whether the man's age is a main idea or a supporting detail. (Answer: supporting detail.)

Encourage students to highlight the relevant points in the text and to read around the points, as the task is impossible to do without knowing the context in which the points are made.

Answers
1 Main ideas: a, c, d. Supporting details: b, e, f.
2 b It's not only English people who are affected by FAS.
  e Germanic or Nordic speakers of English use different vowel sounds from native speakers of English.
  f FAS happens to relatively young people.
3 Although from a textbook, the style isn't too formal or off-putting. In places, the style is quite friendly, almost 'chatty'.

  E.g. 'Apparently this patient enjoyed having an accent and just as well'
    What's going on here? ... or what?'

4 Students can be given the opportunity to analyse their own pronunciation. They scan paragraphs 4 and 6 again to find four main types of pronunciation error. These are:

- mistakes in vowel sounds
- mistakes in consonant sounds
- misplaced stress on words
- inappropriate rhythm and intonation

Encourage students to try to determine their own pronunciation mistakes. With your help, they should be able to decide if their mistakes are typical of their nationality.

Vocabulary development: words for talking about language

1 Students scan the text for vocabulary that relates specifically to pronunciation. Less familiar may be the ones to do with pronunciation (tone, stresses etc.). Ensure students are clear about these words as they will need them for the extension activity.

Answers

> accent
> slurred speech
> speak
> talk
> rhythm
> rising and falling tones
> sing-song
> stress
> vowel sounds

2 Students complete the idioms a–h, paying attention to collocation. Each cartoon represents one of the idioms.

Answers

> a Speak
> b Say
> c talk
> d say
> e Talk
> f Speak
> g talking
> h say

Writing skill: writing a summary

1 Allow students about 15 minutes for Exercise 1.

2 You can help the students to express the ideas in their own words, as paraphrasing is an important skill that students often find problematic.

3 Students complete the task either in class or for homework.

4 Students exchange summaries with a partner and peer-correct.

PART TWO
Sign language (SB page 54)

Lead-in

This is intended to be a light-hearted introduction to the listening comprehension on sign language awareness. Point out that the finger-spelling alphabet is not the same as British sign-language which is actually a language in its own right.

Find out from the students if they know how to communicate using any form of sign language. Students then finger-spell key names/place names to their partner to write down. Obviously they are not allowed to speak.

Listening technique: comprehension and inference

1 Students should be able to complete this part after one listening, correcting statements that are wrong.

Answers

> a F (He fell into working with deaf people.)
> b T
> c T (social work 'wasn't his cup of tea' – find out how this idea is expressed in the students' native language.)
> d T
> e F (He now works in a university.)
> f DS (Doesn't say.)

Listening technique: following instructions

This activity is a little different from all the others in this book. Students demonstrate their comprehension of the listening text by following the instructions that they hear (rather than answering a set of questions, for example).

If the listening activity is exploited fully, the whole class can be involved in miming Peter's instructions, which describe the process of making a cup of tea. You may have to explain that British people usually use a kettle to boil water for tea-making purposes. We have found that students have found the activity fun to do, but obviously if any student feels embarrassed by miming the actions, they should be allowed to sit this one out.

Students will probably appreciate it if you join in this activity. Indeed, we recommend that when Peter says 'I want all of you to stand up' you beckon the students to stand up along with you. Allow some time (a minute or so after Peter has finished speaking) for the students to carry on miming.

After they have finished, elicit from the students:

1 what the aim of the exercise is (i.e. to demonstrate the physical accuracy and ability to visualise mentally what is needed when making signs)
2 whether they think they would make good signers.

Exploring pronunciation: marker words

1 Students listen to extracts from the tape and mark the correct intonation pattern on the underlined words.

Answers

a rising
b falling
c falling
d falling
e rising
f falling
g rising   falling

2 The function of the rising tone is to check the listeners' understanding. When Peter uses a falling tone, he is merely signalling the end of one instruction and the beginning of another. The 'right' or 'okay' acts as a filler.

3 Ask students which words they would use in their own language for each of the two functions: checking understanding and signalling the end of one point and beginning another. Ask them to decide which words they use or would use in English. Encourage students to record these words in the Unit 5 Review page. Point out their usefulness in the Speaking Paper (Section B).

Listening technique: specific information

1 Students listen to the recording of two students attempting an information gap exercise and comment on how well Student A uses marker words.

2 Now students should all cut out the shapes as indicated in the Student's Book and try to follow Student A's instructions. They can check their pattern by referring to page 146.

Speaking skill: giving information to complete a task

Students can now be given the opportunity to try the exercise themselves, rearranging the shapes into a different pattern. Encourage them to use marker words, either to check understanding or to signal that a particular instruction has been completed. Students can also work in groups of three, with one student acting as monitor and making a note of how well each student uses marker words.

Extension activity

These information gap activities can be great fun and students are usually pleasantly surprised to discover that such an activity is included in Paper 5. Such activities are very easy to set up and should be used regularly during the course. In the exam similar but not identical photographs are generally used. However, different materials give equally good practice in the skills of describing, giving

instructions and comparing: these include 'spot the difference' and 'describe and draw' activities. However, it is important that students follow the exam procedure, with Student A speaking for about one minute and Student B then responding.

See **Language awareness: formal and informal language (Page 30)**

EXAM FOCUS: (English in Use, Section B) Informal to formal writing

Rewriting information in a different register is a task that can cause problems for students since it can be quite difficult to decide whether an unfamiliar word is formal or informal. Before attempting this activity, students will benefit from looking at the Language Awareness section on formal and informal language on page 60.

1 Students read the memo and underline examples of informal words and phrases.

Answers

Use of contractions	she's, she'll, doesn't
Missing words out	(it) sounds useful, (I've) Just had a chat
Colloquialisms	all sorts of things, that kind of thing, get hold of
Phrasal verbs	start off, go on to, finish off, get hold of
Use of questions and question tags	Shall we make it next Friday ...? Sounds useful, doesn't it?
Vocabulary	a chat, reckons, a bit

2 Get students to study the gaps in the formal text and find the equivalent information in the informal memo.

a do a talk
b teaching
c about
d all sorts of
e start off
f go on
g (change of grammatical structure needed)
h finish off
i if she's got time
j cost
k to get in
l put on lunch
m get hold of

3 Students complete the announcement by using more formal equivalents.

Answers

a giving/holding	h conclude
b educating	i enough/sufficient
c approximately	j charge
d various	k admission
e begin/commence	l be provided
f be/follow	m contact
g After	

PART THREE
Body language (SB page 57)

Lead-in

1 Students discuss the possible meanings for each of the gestures.

Answers

(From left to right)
Winking: 'It's a secret.' / 'I'm joking.'
Finger to temple (and rotating): 'He/she's crazy.'
Tapping nose: 'Mind your own business.' / 'I'm not going to tell you.'

2 Ask students to list some important gestures that tourists to their country should be aware of. Clearly, this activity needs to be tackled sensitively. Care should be taken in a multilingual group not to cause offence. In addition, the level of maturity of the class may necessitate avoiding the activity completely.

Reading technique: scanning

To give the students an added reason to read, you could ask them to imagine they are flying to an international conference as delegates from all the countries listed in the chart. They discover the article on body language in the in-flight magazine five minutes before the plane is due to land.

1 Encourage students to time themselves for this activity, reminding them if necessary how important speed reading is in the real world, as well as for the exam. Emphasise that they should not worry about unknown words yet, apart from the ones they may need to perform the task, which they can cross-check in pairs if necessary.

Answers

Touching lower eyelid
Saudi Arabia ✗   South America ✓ or ✗
Tugging ear lobe
Spain ✗   Greece ✗   Portugal ✓   Malta ✗
Thumbs up
Sardinia ✗   Britain ✓

2 Students scan the advertisement and find the four different meanings for the ring gesture.

Answers

'A-OK' – America
'money' – Japan
'I'll kill you' – Tunisia
'zero' – France

Vocabulary development: guessing unknown words

Students match the words or phrases with the correct definitions. Stress the importance of finding the words in their correct context.

Answers

1 g	5 a
2 e	6 h
3 i	7 d
4 b	8 j

See Language awareness: expressing time (page 61)

Speaking skill: giving a talk

1–2 Students examine the list and categorise the points as either good or bad (although they may want to qualify some of the points). It will be interesting in a multicultural group to look for points of disagreement; for example, the Japanese dislike of direct eye contact may influence their view of 'looking directly at the audience'. Students then discuss the effect that nerves might have with regard to the list of points.

3 Students think of a topic that they can give a talk on. Make it clear that this activity is not a test of knowledge but merely the opportunity to practise the skill of extended speaking. Students could talk about a hobby, national pastimes, a memorable holiday or any subject they feel confident about. Insist that they make notes and do not simply write a speech, but encourage them to use the expressions listed in order to structure their talk. They can give their talk to a small group to avoid intimidating less confident students. Invite the students in the group to comment on each speaker's fluency, accuracy, pronunciation, content, etc.

Extension activity

If you want to give your students time to prepare a more formal presentation (possibly with visual aids) to give to the whole class, then this can be prepared for the next lesson. If you have a large class, the students can work in pairs to give a joint presentation. If the students are willing and you have recording facilities in your school or institution, you could film a number of the talks and play them back for whole class feedback/error analysis. Always remember to emphasise good points as well as weak ones.

You can use the following feedback sheet, or design your own.

Name:

Topic:

Was the talk clear, easy to follow and interesting?

Was the language used accurate? Note down any language errors.

Was the speaker fluent or a little hesitant at times?

Was the speaker's body language appropriate?

LANGUAGE AWARENESS: formal and informal language

This activity provides students with a summary of some of the main language features of formal and informal language. A crucial skill for CAE is for the candidates to be able to move across different registers in their writing.

1 Students read the two letters and underline the words or phrases that are examples of formal and informal language. Try to elicit categories rather than simply individual lexical items, as this will help students to make informed choices in the future.

2 Having examined the two letters, ask the students to draw a chart with the 10 features and to fill it in with examples from the texts.

Answers

	Formal	Informal
Idiomatic English	Not used	Commonly used e.g. the long and the short of it
Phrasal verbs	Avoided e.g. on arrival; to be reimbursed	Commonly used e.g. when we turned up; to pay me back
Understatement	Commonly used e.g. I was rather disappointed...; take further action*	More direct e.g. I was furious!; taking them to court
Contractions	Usually avoided	Commonly used e.g. they'd, I'd
Missing out words	Not used	Commonly used e.g. (this is) just a quick note...
Passives	Commonly used e.g. my room had been given to ...	Less common e.g. they'd given our room ... (active voice)
Punctuation	Exclamation marks and dashes avoided	Question marks, dashes, exclamation marks commonly used
Inversion (grammatical structures)	Commonly used e.g. Should I receive no satisfaction, ...	Not used
Vocabulary	e.g. alternative accommodation; consequently Full forms of words e.g. television, telephone	e.g. another room; anyway Clipped forms e.g. telly, phone
Length of sentences	Longer. Sentences often include non-defining relative clauses, use of linking words like 'despite the fact', 'moreover'	Shorter

* Understatement is often used in formal writing when giving advice or complaining.

3 Remind students to keep a record of contrasting stylistic features in the formal/informal Record Sheet on page 147.

4 There are many pairs of equivalent words in English which have similar meanings but are different in terms of register or formality. Historically, it is the words which come from Anglo-Saxon which nowadays are regarded as informal or colloquial words. These can be contrasted with words which have come into the language via French or Latin which tend to have retained a more formal air. For example:

Anglo-Saxon	French or Latin
before	preceding
burn	incinerate
funny	amusing
stop	cease

As a general rule of thumb, formal words tend to be longer.

Students try to find matching pairs from the list. This is a simple exercise designed to raise awareness rather than build new vocabulary.

Answers

(Informal first)
ask – enquire
tell – inform
gear – equipment
talk – converse
children – offspring
go – proceed
buy – purchase
car – vehicle

Point out that particular vocabulary items cannot be labelled simply as 'formal' or 'informal'. Rather, encourage students to look at the context of the word in general.

5 Students supply the appropriate formal or informal words for the gaps in the sentences. Ensure that they use the correct tense for the context.

Answers

a consumed
b buy
c informed
d children
e vehicles
f conversing
g gear
h proceed

LANGUAGE AWARENESS: expressing time

1 Students try to work out the answer to the puzzle.

Answer

They were both exercising in a gym.

2 Students re-read the text and decide on the sequence of actions in the following sentences. The use of past perfect and present perfect in the second and third sentences shows that one action was/will be completed before the other.

Answer

When Sharon looked at her watch she noticed it wasn't working. (A)
Once they'd rested for a few minutes, Sharon decided to do some more running. (B)
When we've finished I'll meet you in the changing room. (B)
When Sharon started running, Tracy started cycling. (A)

3 Students complete the general rule as follows:

Answer

When one action is the result of another, or one action happens immediately after another, you should use the past simple in both clauses. If you want to emphasise that one action was (will be) completed before another one began (begins) you should use the past perfect or the present perfect to describe the first action.

4 Students examine the pairs of statements and decide which one in each case corresponds to the sequence of events in the puzzle. Point out that this activity serves to revise past tenses as well as to practise use of time conjunctions.

Answers

1 b
2 c
3 e
4 g
5 i

5 Students rewrite the incorrect sentences using the given time adverbials.

Answers

a Once they had changed into their kit they started jogging

d By the time Sharon looked at her watch it had stopped

f After Sharon had rested for a few minutes she decided to do some more running

h They didn't start running and cycling until they had decided to meet again

j As soon as Sharon started running, Tracy started cycling

6 Students read the dialogue and decide how many times Tom contradicts Steve. This can be worked out by the use of tenses and time adverbials.

Answers

Four times:
- It drove past when we'd left the house
- Yeah, we remembered we'd forgotten it by the time we got on the bus.
- Yeah, we'd decided when we sat down.
- Yes, sir. We talked about what we should tell you until we got to school

Hopefully, one of the sharper students will point out the other contradiction: the use of 'how' and 'what' in the last exchange.

7 Students rewrite the incorrect sentences, using different time conjunctions from the ones used by Steve. Some statements have more than one answer; however, the most natural are offered below. Point out that the past perfect is only used when any ambiguity exists.

Answers

- While we were leaving the house/When we left the house the bus drove past.
- We didn't remember we'd forgotten it until we got on the bus.
- We decided after we'd sat down.
- We talked about how we should tell you after we got to school.

Food and Drink

PART ONE
Garlic (SB page 63)

Lead-in

Treat this brief lead-in as a whole class discussion. Discuss whether garlic is used commonly in the students' own countries for cooking or other purposes. Explain that the English tend to be rather uncomfortable about cooking with garlic (due to worry about the smell of it on one's breath afterwards!) and until recently it was an ingredient seldom found in the average English kitchen. Elicit from the students some of the positive attributes of garlic (it is thought to be an aphrodisiac and is beneficial to the immune system and the bronchial system).

EXAM FOCUS: (Listening, Section D) extracts for global understanding

This is the first listening activity that aims to provide practice for Section D of Paper 4. Students use lexical clues in the various extracts to identify the occupation of each speaker. Note that in the exam, the candidates have to perform two tasks relating to the same extracts. (See Units 8 and 12 for examples.) Encourage students to look at the list A – F before listening, in order to help them focus their attention.

1 Good students will be able to note down some of the salient words or phrases during the listening. (This is as much a vocabulary-building exercise as a listening.)

Answers

> Suggested key words are in brackets.
> 1 B (book, recipe, soup, ingredients, cooked, boiled, baked, oven, flavour, taste)
> 2 H (film makers/industry)
> 3 C (stay tuned, show, a Mr Hayes of London)
> 4 A (medicinal purposes, treatment, wounds, antiseptic, cholesterol, blood circulation, heart disease, patients, remedy)
> 5 E (house, family, supermarket)

Make sure students have matched the extracts correctly, but delay the checking of words/phrases until they listen a second time (see below).

Listening technique: specific information

Students listen to the text again in order to get specific information, using the photographs as prompts. They should also be able to add more to their lists of words/phrases. Treat this as a student-centred vocabulary exercise, encouraging students to record words which are useful or relevant to them.

Answers

> a Garlic used as a defence against vampires
> b Parsley used to counteract smell of garlic on breath
> c Garlic is beneficial to the heart
> d Description of garlic bread, they buy it from the supermarket
> e Large amount of garlic needed for soup

Reading technique: predicting

Students can work individually or in pairs. The questions serve as an awareness-raiser for the second listening text.

1–4 Students read the first paragraph of a newspaper article and predict the theme of the text. Then they confirm their answers and predict reasons for the writer's failure to grow garlic successfully. Extend discussion to the whole class and write their suggestions on the board (these can be checked/confirmed after the listening).

Listening technique: specific information

Students listen once and correct the writer's mistakes. This should be relatively easy, as the writer clearly 'signposts' his points (e.g. 'I made three big mistakes'). Students can also check their predictions at this stage.

Answers

> 1 Buy garlic from a specialist supplier – best suited to the British climate.
> 2 Plant garlic in autumn – needs cool, damp weather for plant to develop roots.
> 3 Harvest in July – May too early.
> 4 Leave to dry out for a year in direct sunlight and non-humid atmosphere – to prevent disease.

Vocabulary development: collocations

Elicit from students the need to express uncountable food and drink items in terms of measures or containers.

Answers

1 Measures: pint, clove, knob, pinch, sprig
   Containers: carton, pot, bottle, jar

2 • a pint of milk/beer/water* (*e.g. as an ingredient)
   • a clove of garlic (cf. Spanish 'tooth' of garlic – ask students for the equivalent collocation in their native language)
   • a knob of butter
   • a carton of milk/yoghurt
   • a pinch of salt
   • a pot of jam/yoghurt
   • a sprig of parsley
   • a bottle of water/beer/milk
   • a jar of jam

Extension activity

Further examples of similar collocations are given below. These can be jumbled up, with students matching appropriate vocabulary. Ask students to explore any collocations in their own language.

   • a tube of toothpaste/tomato purée
   • a bar of soap/chocolate
   • a box of chocolates/matches
   • a slice of bread/cake
   • a packet of crisps/biscuits

3 Students make a note of collocations that can be reversed.

Answers

a beer/milk/water bottle
a milk/yoghurt carton
a jam/yoghurt pot
a jam jar

Elicit from the students the fact that we use the preposition structure (with 'of') to talk about a container with its contents inside, whereas the compound structure refers to the type of container itself, not necessarily with its contents.

4 **Pronunciation tip**: students will often make the mistake of giving unstressed words (in this case, 'a' and 'of') their full stress.

Writing skill: describing a process (formal)

1 Ask students to consider the writer's use of the active voice. Try to elicit the fact that the effect is to give the listener a greater sense of involvement – as though we are being addressed directly.

2 Students work in pairs to explore more formal language needed to write a paragraph on the correct process of growing garlic. If students need help, suggest that they refer back to the Language Awareness section on use of the passive on page 49.

   Useful connectors:
   • First of all, ...
   • The next stage is ...
   • It is important to remember ...
   • Furthermore, ...

3 Students complete the writing task individually in class time. When finished they swap with a partner and correct each other's work, using the marking criteria supplied in the Student's Book.

PART TWO
Drink (SB page 67)

Lead-in

We feel that it is important to give a sufficient amount of time to this activity (at least 15 minutes) in order that students have the chance to air their feelings about alcohol, particularly those students who may have moral, cultural or religious objections to drink.

One way of exploring associations of particular words is to present them in the form of a mind-map. Students can then present their maps to others in the group. After 10 minutes or so of group discussion, you can ask one person in each group to report to the whole class.

Extension activity

Students might find the following vocabulary useful, particulary those who intend to visit Britain on business or as tourists. Write the following words and phrases on the board and ask the students if they know or can guess the meanings.

• What's yours? (What would you like to drink?)
• Cheers! (A toast when drinking)
• It's my round. (It's my turn to buy everyone a drink)

- I'll have a short please – a large one! (I'll have a spirit please – a double!)
- Excuse me, my beer's flat! (My beer isn't very gassy)
- Whose shout is it? (Whose turn is it to buy a drink?)
- Time, gentlemen (sic) please. (Time to go home – said by the bar staff at closing time.)

Reading technique: skimming

In order for students to develop the habit of skim-reading, we suggest that they have only one minute for this activity. If they look out for the words in the previous activity, they should have little problem in identifying the writer's main concern.

Answer
Beer and wine

Reading technique: information transfer

1–2 This activity may provide a stimulating challenge for adult students who do not often have the chance to show off their skills in subjects other than their knowledge of English! Useful vocabulary will depend on whether students choose a basic bar chart (x/horizontal axis; y/vertical axis; scale) or the more complicated pie chart (where they will need to calculate percentages). Draw attention to the diagrams in the the Student's Book which give an idea of the kind of results you might expect.

3 When students have finished their diagrams they can complete the notes underneath.

Vocabulary development: using synonyms

1 The text provides students with an opportunity to see how good writers make use of synonymous words and phrases, a process referred to by linguists as 'lexical chaining'. However, students need to be aware of the different levels of formality of these synonyms, and the following activities should alert them to the dangers of transferring these words to other contexts which may not be appropriate.

2–3 Students locate the equivalent phrases and then complete the chart.

Formal	Neutral	Colloquial
is better suited to	grow better in	
	beer	brew
	drink	tipple
	has become more readily available in	has invaded (metaphorical)
Soviet consumption had fallen to	the average Russian citizen drank	

Exploring pronunciation: vowel sounds

This activity is designed to focus on the tricky area of pronunciation of vowel sounds for non-native speakers of English.

1 The words selected illustrate very clearly the poor link between English spelling and pronunciation!

Answers
1 d, e
2 b, f
3 a, h
4 c, g

2–3 Students write their own activity to test each other.

EXAM FOCUS: (Writing Section B) a letter to an international magazine

This activity replicates a typical Section B writing question. Encourage students to work together in the initial stage, in which they clarify what is meant by the question and generate ideas about what to write. As usual, let the students write a first draft in class and complete a final version at home.

Extension activity
A discussion or even a formal debate can be organised around the issue of alcohol. Many issues can be covered, including:

- drinking and driving
- addiction
- under-age drinking (in France, children of all ages are permitted to drink wine in small amounts; compare this to the legislation in many countries that tries to restrict under-age drinking)
- alcohol-related violence (a problem in Britain and America)
- prohibition (using America earlier this century as an example of what can go wrong)

PART THREE
The hamburger empire (SB page 70)

Lead-in

1 As an introduction to the quiz, ask students what their experience of foreign food is: what have they tried, and did they like it? (Popular 'foreign' foods in Britain presently are Indian, Chinese, Italian and, more recently, Thai and Mexican.) Keep this short; a couple of minutes should be sufficient.

2–3 Divide students into groups of three or four. Obviously, in a mixed-nationality class students may prefer to organise themselves to have a range of nationalities within each group, and enhance their chances! In our experience, students find quizzes such as these great fun and highly motivating. You could offer a small prize (to do with food?) in order to add even more of a competitive element to the quiz.

Answers

1 meat and salad (tomato, cucumber, tzatziki, onion) wrapped inside pitta bread (a Middle Eastern flat bread)
2 raw fish
3 cooking pan commonly used for Oriental food (e.g. stir-frying)
4 cereal, toast, mixed grill (choice of bacon, mushrooms, tomatoes, egg, sausages)
5 a type of flat bread eaten with Indian food
6 Hungary
7 Spain
8 A popular fast-food restaurant, or a type of meal eaten in that restaurant. (as in 'Let's go for a McDonald's')

Students could finally devise their own questions and test opposing groups.

Speaking skill: sharing information

1–2 When we talk about food across the world it is very easy to think in terms of stereotyped meals (e.g. English fish and chips!). Students spend around 10 minutes discussing their respective national dishes, and whether they will still have any significance in the future. Try to get them not pre-empt too much of the discussion scheduled for the next session on fast-food restaurants abroad.

Reading technique: summary skills

1 Students work to match the paragraph to the best summary. If they find this tricky, encourage them to share answers with others before checking with you.

Answers

1 C
2 G
3 F
4 D
5 I
6 A

2 Students imagine what could have been said about the remaining points, namely B, E and H. For example:

B The role of fast food in a healthy diet. (Is all fast food unhealthy? Or are health and fast food contradictory ideas? If so, why? Tap into the students' own knowledge here.)

E Local objections to McDonald's (e.g. from local restauranteurs, environmentalists).

H McDonald's as a major employer (What types of people? How old are they? How long do they stay with the company?

This will encourage students to think about some of the points which will be used in the next session (they should keep their notes for this reason).

Reading technique: understanding the purpose of a text

These questions focus on the writer's purpose, genre, and attitude. You can remind students that in Paper 1, there is usually at least one multiple choice question of the type that asks for an understanding of the purpose, the style or the writer's attitude.

Answers

1 B (Although there is some criticsm implied in the final paragraph, the main purpose is merely to give an account of McDonald's success abroad.)
2 B (The source is actually The Journal of Geography.)
3 C (The writer makes no value judgements about the spread of McDonald's.)

Extension activity

Students rewrite a paragraph of the text in the style of either a tabloid newspaper or an environmentalist leaflet. It will help if some examples of these can be shown to them as models.

See **Language awareness: participles 1**

Vocabulary development: recording vocabulary

1–2 This should be a collaborative exercise, aiming to encourage good vocabulary-recording skills. (This might be a good time for students to check each other's Review pages for the units so far, and to compare the various ways of recording vocabulary.)

In class, they should focus only on the meanings of the words in the context given. However, by all means advise them to check other meanings, at home. A good way to test for collocations is to ask native speakers (if students have access to them) about their own intuitions.

Suggested collocations:
a brief respite
minor/small/major/mutual concessions
a barrage of criticisms/questions

Speaking skill: taking part in a debate

We hope that students will find this topic a stimulating one. The debate can be organised in a formal way with the chairperson handling the introduction of the speakers, the question-and-answer session and the voting at the end. You should try not to intervene at all during the debate: Your role can be to act as monitor for language errors, which can be discussed and explained afterwards.

Extension activity

Students can argue for or against the motion that some of their most treasured/popular national dishes could be served on a fast-food basis. This could also be organised on the basis of a business plan – would it be a feasible project? This could prove very informative in a multilingual group, especially with students whose countries offer examples of 'hole in the wall' or street vendors who sell tasty, high-quality fast food! Would these culinary tastes go down well in other countries? The authors are convinced that Greek 'souvlakis' (see the beginning of Part 3) would prove tough competition for our own fish and chip shops!

LANGUAGE AWARENESS:
Participles (1)

1 Students comment on the student's mistake in the cartoon.

Answer

The student used the present participle 'boring' instead of the past participle 'bored'. This is a comment on his personality rather than his feelings!

2 Students supply the appropriate participle in each sentence.

Answers

a disappointed/terrified/shocked/worried
b disappointing/worrying
c embarrassing
d excited/worried
e irritating
f astounding
g enthralling
h tempted

3 Students form as many compound adjectives as possible using words from column A and B. Encourage them to make use of a good dictionary.

Answers

narrow-minded
wide-eyed
empty-handed
full-grown
big-headed
small-minded
long-sighted, long-playing, long-winded
short-sighted
heavy-handed
light-headed
high-powered, high-minded, high-flying
near-sighted
low-flying, low-lying
far-fetched, far-reaching, far-sighted

4 Students supply an appropriate compound adjective from their list to complete each sentence.

Answers

a empty-handed
b short-sighted, near-sighted
c far-reaching
d narrow-minded
e big-headed
f high-flying, high-powered
g low-lying

LANGUAGE AWARENESS: expressing possibility

1 Students read the dialogue and underline all the structures that express degrees of possibility, putting them in the appropriate section of the table.

Answers

	certain ◄————————► possible		
Past	can't have	must have	might have/ could have
Present	can't be	should be	might be
Future	won't will be		might

2–3 Students try to work out the answer to the puzzle, rewriting each sentence using an appropriate modal verb. This activity is designed to offer students examples of informal vocabulary used to express degrees of possibility and to practise present, past and future forms. Students will need to use a good dictionary to look up the definitions of words or expressions like 'to be bound to', 'to bet' and 'to be odds on', for which there may be more than one answer.

Answers

a He must have had a heart attack.
b He might/could have been robbed.
c He can't have been robbed ...
d He might/could be meditating!
e It must have been an accident.
f There must be a very logical explanation.
g The bag will/must have something to do with it.
h He must have been flying ...
i The local flying club will be looking for him.
j He won't/can't have checked his parachute.

4 In pairs students try to decide the reason for the situation in the picture, namely why the man is dead. Insist that they follow the instructions in the Student's Book carefully, covering up the clues and only revealing the next one when they have written down their deduction on a piece of paper. Students should be encouraged to use some of the informal vocabulary they have learned, as well as modal structures.

The Human Condition

PART ONE
A gifted child (SB page 76)

Lead-in

1 Students attempt the test. This is a light-hearted exercise but it might be more interesting if students discover this for themselves.

Answers

a This should be done in the square at the bottom, not the rectangle!

b All of them.

c 70.

d Half-way. After the mid-way point the dog is running out of the forest.

e Peacocks don't lay eggs.

f The match.

g He shouldn't really be buried if he's still living!

h For there to be a widow the man must have died.

2 Students discuss any particular skills or talents they had as children. What was the first book they read? Did they have any particular talents as children that they failed to develop further or simply lost interest in?

3 Students discuss and estimate ages for a person of an average ability. Although this serves as a prediction exercise for the following pre-listening task, other skills could be included to encourage further discussion. Alternatively, students could discuss the various skills children would be expected to aquire from the ages of two to seven (the ages of the children in the extracts).

4 Students read the extracts and check their ideas. Explain that the children are now grown up and encourage students to discuss the possible careers they followed.

Extension activity

This activity can act as a lead-in to the listening as well as offering a chance to generate ideas for the writing activity later in this section. Students select the answers that come closest to their own opinions and discuss their views in pairs or groups.

Parents should:

a push their child to achieve the highest degree of success.

b ignore or discourage their child's special talent.

c seek publicity for their child.

d encourage but not pressurise their child to use their talent.

Gifted children should:

a be educated at home by parents or by private tutors.

b be treated exactly the same at school as other children.

c be given extra homework.

d be moved up to a higher class.

Socially, gifted children should be encouraged to mix:

a with children of their own age.

b with other gifted children.

c with older children or adults.

d only with family members.

Listening technique: specific information

Students listen to the tape once and fill in a table like the one in the Student's Book. Allow students to compare answers.

Answers

Stephanie Peters
Housewife; parents didn't pressurise her but had high expectations of her; over-confidence; laziness leading to problems at university; intimidating members of the opposite sex; feeling shy.

Everton Williams
Unemployed; parents disappointed; feeling under pressure; hating books; getting bullied at school; not settling in to a new school; left at 16; difficulties relating to people who he finds boring.

Jamie Sutton
Insurance salesman; father pushed him to excel at music to the detriment of everything else; being educated at home meant he missed out on some things like sports and an interest in pop music; had less time to make friends.

Listening technique: inference

1   Students listen a second time, listing the problems these people faced as a consequence of their early abilities. Again, allow students to compare ideas and, if necessary, to listen again before you ask for responses.

Answers

Stephanie Peters
seems very happy

Everton Williams
seems a little unhappy

Jamie Sutton
seems very happy

Vocabulary development: collocation

1   The importance of collocation can be pointed out to students with a few simple examples.

E.g.   A person can be tall or short but hair is long or short.
A person can be young or old but a car would be new or old.

Students fill in the chart, ticking the possible collocations and using dictionaries if available.

Answers

good	all
gifted	all
fluent	speaker
skilled	artist, musician
agile	athlete
clever	possibly none of them. But this is open to discussion.
efficient	business person
talented	athlete, artist, musician, business person
shrewd	business person
astute	business person

2   Students discuss the meanings of these different words.

Answers

good	having positive qualities
gifted	having a natural ability or talent
fluent	having the ability to speak or write smoothly and accurately
skilled	having acquired ability, usually manual
agile	having the ability to move quickly and easily
clever	good at learning (more likely to be used to describe a child than an adult)
efficient	able to work well, especially as regards time
talented	having (a natural) ability in something
shrewd	having good judgement or common sense, especially in business
astute	having insight, able to assess situations easily

3   Students discuss similar collocations in their own language.

Writing skill: an article for a newsletter

1   Students either listen to the tape again or turn to the tapescript, and list the benefits/problems of being a gifted child. Then they can work backwards to find the action and consider a benefit and a problem that could ensue from this action. They will benefit from working with others for this activity. You could even extend it to a whole class discussion, with you writing all their points on the board.

2   Ask students to comment on how the example paragraph has been organised, (i.e. action/benefit/problem). Ask them to think of words or phrases used to describe cause and effect (a good selection are listed in the Student's Book). Write one of the causes and a related effect on the board, if you haven't already done so, and ask students to link these together using any of the cause and effect phrases. Monitor for accuracy here.

Allow students time to discuss the use of further linking devices. When they feel confident in using these, encourage groups to examine the different ways the newsletter could be organised. They should also consider who the audience is for this newsletter. Let students decide which level of formality would be most suitable for this task.

3   Individual students work on the first part of the article before they compare their writing with that of others. Encourage them to give practical feedback in terms of language and/or content. The whole group should discuss solutions to the problems raised by each of the students before

they proceed to the second part. Remind students of the phrases for giving advice in Unit 1, Part One. The article can be completed for homework, as long as the preparation is done in class.

PART TWO
Memory (SB page 79)

1 Students examine the various revision methods and discuss which ones apply to them.

2 Explain that the students are going to read an article giving advice on good and bad revision methods. They should now decide which of the points listed are recommended and which are not. This will give them the opportunity to justify their own revision methods, some of which may appear rational (like listening to music) but which the article argues against.

Reading technique: skimming

Divide the class into two groups. Group A should read text 1, group B text 2. Allow students one minute only to skim-read their text: they should concentrate simply on finding out how many of the points are dealt with in their text. Some of the points appear in both.

Answers

Text 1	Text 2
a, c, e, f, g, h	b, d, e,

Reading technique: specific information

1 Students re-read their text, making notes under the relevant points. Insist on notes rather than full sentences or chunks copied from the text. This will allow for a far more communicative activity later, when students share information.

2 When everyone is finished, students from each group form pairs and share their information.

3 Students share ideas on revision methods. Is the advice given in the article suitable for language students?

Extension activity

This would be an opportune moment to discuss learner training techniques and methods for self-study. Some important points are listed here.

- Extensive reading for vocabulary development
- Intensive reading of extracts from newspaper or magazine articles for language awareness practice
- Practice in listening that allows for global and specific understanding.
- Proofreading other students' written work
- Recording group discussions for analysis of fluency, accuracy and pronunciation

See Language awareness: verb forms (1) (page 42)

EXAM FOCUS: (English in Use, Section B) proofreading

Students read the extract and decide which lines contain a word that is either grammatically incorrect or which does not fit in with the sense of the text.

Answers

The following words should not be included:

1 had	6 ✓	11 with
2 so	7 quite	12 who
3 in	8 ✓	13 that
4 when	9 rather	14 for
5 not	10 ✓	

Speaking skill: describing in detail

1 Divide the class into two groups. Students work together to give the people in their pictures names, personalities and jobs and to decide the possible relationships between them.

2 Students then write a list of questions (at least seven) based on their descriptions. These will later be used to test their partner's memory.

3 Students pair up with somebody from the opposite group. Having described the people in their picture, they test their partner's memory with their prepared questions. Encourage students to use the expressions listed in the Student's Book when describing.

PART THREE
Phobias (SB page 82)

Lead-in

1–2 Students read the extract from George Orwell's '1984', then decide what would be in their Room 101. Students can discuss which of the fears mentioned in the text and shown in the pictures can be regarded as rational and which as irrational.

3 This activity is designed to focus attention on Greek affixes. Students match the descriptions with their proper names. (g will probably be done by elimination).

Answers

a arachnophobia
b toxiphobia
c hydrophobia
d photophobia
e geraphobia
f opthalmophobia
g belonephobia
h hypnophobia

4–5 Students discuss these questions in pairs as an awareness-raising for the Exam Focus which follows.

EXAM FOCUS: (Listening, Section C) making notes

1–3 Make sure that students read through the advice sheet first to encourage their ability to anticipate crucial information. Point out that no more than three words should be used. After listening (twice if necessary), you can discuss useful listening strategies with students.

Suggested answers

A embarrassment
B disrupt your life
C going outside
D air travel/flying
E buttons and beards
F in a cupboard
G an anaesthetic
H equally likely
I drugs
J acupuncture
K qualified professional

See Language awareness: will, would and used to (page 43)

Vocabulary development: word building

If students are able to recognise many of the common Latin and Greek elements that are or have been used to create words in English, this will give them a valuable tool in working out probable meanings.

1 Let students organise themselves into groups for the first part of this activity. The roots most likely to generate words in English are as follows:

Root	Examples
hypno-	hypnosis, hypnotist (note different stress)
gera-	geriatric (note spelling change)
opthalmo-	opthalmic
pyro-	pyromania, pyrotechnics

As a light-hearted extension, you could let students generate nonsense words and definitions.

2
Answers

ambi-	both
ante-	before
anti-	against
circa-	about, around
micro-	small
peri-	around

3 Students work in groups to add others to the list.

LANGUAGE AWARENESS: verb forms (1)

This section looks at three uses of the gerund or '-ing' form of the verb:

a when the verb form acts as a noun
   E.g.   Bringing boring information to life can help you remember information.

b when the verb follows a preposition
   E.g.   Some students are in the habit of leaving revision until the last moment.

c after certain verbs
   E.g.   Don't risk leaving revision until the last moment.

1 Students look at the extracts and explain the use of the gerund. They may well need assistance in discovering that each extract is acting as the subject. It will be very beneficial at this stage to practise creating similar structures. Sentences beginning with a simple noun can be written on the board and students asked to extend them.

E.g.   Televison can be educational.
       Watching certain programmes on the tele-
       vision can be educational.
       The CAE exam is challenging.
       Studying for the CAE exam is challenging.

2 Students rewrite each sentence using the gerund
form as the subject of the sentence.

Answers

> a Forgetting things you haven't understood is
>   common.
> b Preparing answers to particular questions is
>   not a good idea.
> c Recalling facts from material learnt over a long
>   time takes less effort.
> d Remembering something that fascinates you
>   is easier.

3 Students rewrite sentences using verbs from box
A, a preposition from box B and a suitable gerund
form. Before students attempt these, elicit the
reason for the gerund in the example – that the
verb follows a preposition.

Answers

> Manuela's afraid of failing her exams.
> Phillip insisted on paying me.
> Katie was good at driving.
> The teacher didn't apologise for arriving late.
> Jenny is in the habit of turning up uninvited.
> I was angry at missing the party.
> Some people don't care about upsetting others.
> Many people dream of retiring early.

4 Students decide which of the eight sentences are
incorrect and why.

Answers

> Incorrect sentences: 1, 3, 5, 6, 7, 8.
>
> Sentences 1, 3, 5 and 8 contain verbs that take
> the gerund. Sentences 6 and 7 contain verbs
> that take 'to' + infinitive.

5 Students should be able to give three reasons for
using the gerund:

- when the verb is used as a noun
- when the verb follows a preposition
- after certain verbs

Point out that knowledge of verb forms is particularly important in the English in Use paper,
Section C.

LANGUAGE AWARENESS:
will, would and used to

1 Students begin by listing all the uses of 'will' and
'would' that they can think of, giving examples of
each.

2 Students match the uses with the 10 example
sentences. They should be encouraged to define
any that remain.

Answers

I'll be home about 6.00.	prediction
I'm sure she'll give you a lift home.	willingness
Grandfather would always bring me	past habits
She will insist on smoking	criticism (stressed 'will')
Is that the phone? I'll answer it.	offering
Will you give me a hand?	request
... this woman would be his wife.	future in the past
You would do that, wouldn't you?	criticism (stressed)
I'd like a cup of tea.	request
I wouldn't if I were you.	advice

3 Students decide on the use of 'would' in the
extract.

Answer

> Past (characteristic) habit

4 Students decide in which of the two extracts this
form of 'would' can be used. Some students may
have problems distinguishing past states from
past habits. However, it will be more beneficial if
they discover any mistakes for themselves when
they proofread each other's work.

Answers

> b, c, f

5 Students read the magazine extract and write a
short paragraph in which they describe some
fond childhood memories, using 'used to' and
'would' appropriately.

UNIT 8

Leisure

PART ONE
Armchair entertainment (SB page 87)

Lead-in

Students work together to sort out the words into the relevant category as a vocabulary development exercise. Help them with any unfamiliar words.

Answers

Books
- complete works (e.g. of Shakespeare)
- blockbuster
- comic novel
- autobiography
- Mills and Boon romance (the most famous publisher of romantic fiction in Britain)
- whodunnit (a crime story where the main storyline revolves around finding the murderer – who 'done' it)
- thriller
- new edition

Films
- blockbuster
- comedy
- (spaghetti) western
- sequel
- whodunnit
- remake
- weepie (type of film which plays excessively on one's emotions with the intention of making the viewer weep)
- thriller
- cartoon
- cult movie (type of film which has a restricted audience, as opposed to a mainstream appeal)

Television
- soap opera (usually shortened to 'soap')
- chat-show (a presenter interviews famous people)
- documentary (factual programme about topical issues)
- telethon (televised charity appeal where viewers are encouraged to make donations by phone)
- repeat
- sitcom (or 'situation comedy' – usually a 30-minute comedy based around everyday situations such as family or work)

Encourage the students to give examples of these types. It could be fruitful to compare 'home-grown' programmes/films/literature with American or English 'imports'.

Extension activity
Put the students into larger groups (6+) and ask them to agree or disagree with the following statements:

- I prefer to see a film at the cinema rather than on TV or on video.
- I like to read about movies and film stars.
- I prefer off-beat and cult movies to Hollywood blockbusters.
- When a film is made out of a book the result is usually disappointing.
- I try to be selective in my viewing of TV.
- I don't usually have much time to read for pleasure.
- I'm more of a telly addict than a bookworm.

EXAM FOCUS: (Listening Section D) Identifying topics and opinions

1 This replicates Section D of the Listening paper in which students listen to five extracts and have to identify the various topics being talked about, and/or the speakers or their opinions. Before the students listen for the first time, emphasise the importance of reading the various categories so they can anticipate the information they are going to hear.

2 Play the tape a second time and this time the students focus their attention on the opinions expressed by the speakers. You may want to explain the words 'uninformative' and 'uplifting' if these words are problematic for your students (as they were for some of ours!).

3 Encourage students to share their answers with each other before you give them the right ones. They may want to look at the tapescript for answers which were incorrect, so allow a couple of minutes for this.

Answers

1

1 e	4 a
2 g	5 f
3 c	

2

1 d	4 g
2 b	5 c
3 a	

Reading technique: skimming

Set a time limit of around four minutes for this exercise. Students skim-read the texts to find out which genre each book or film belongs to.

Answers

A *The Joy Luck Club* – weepie
B *Century* – period drama/romance
C *Charlotte Brontë: A passionate life* – biography
D *Lovers and Liars* – thriller/blockbuster
E *The 39 Steps* – comedy thriller

Reading technique: scanning and inferring

Students have to apply the skills of searching for explicit information as well as reading between the lines. Students should work together to compare their answers.

Answers

1

a A ('every mother and daughter should see this film')
b D, E
c A, B, C
d A, D
e B, C, D, E

2 Absolutely not! A key feature of authentic reviews is that they don't spoil the ending for the reader. Make sure students bear this in mind when writing their own reviews.

Writing skill: the language of reviews

The aim of this activity is to help the students to write an authentic-style book or film review.

1 The first activity is designed to focus students' attention on some of the common language features of magazine reviews, namely the economical use of language, and the use of the present tense to narrate the plot.

Preferred answers

b, a, b, b, a

3 Let students work in small groups for this activity although the writing should be done on an individual basis. As usual, encourage the students to exchange first drafts in class time and let them write a neat version for homework. There is a sample student answer on page 151 of the Student's Book.

PART TWO
Sport (SB page 90)

Lead-in

Again this lead-in aims to build topic vocabulary. Put the students into groups and allow at least 10 minutes for this activity.

Answers

a referees – football, rugby, hockey
   umpires – tennis, cricket
b competition – more serious than a contest in which two or more people take part
   contest – often a 'one-off' competition, usually (but not always) between two people
   championship – series of games or events in which individuals or teams compete to become overall champion
c prize – award given to the winner of a competition (e.g. first prize, second prize)
   trophy – object awarded as a prize (e.g. Wimbledon tennis trophy, FA Cup)
   title – label given to the winner of a competition (e.g. boxing: world heavyweight title)
d a track – athletics
   a ring – boxing
   a pitch – football, rugby, hockey, baseball
   a court – tennis, badminton, squash, basketball, netball, volleyball
   a rink – ice-skating, ice-hockey

   Note that all of these can be expressed as compounds (e.g. ice-skating rink, running track).
e (anti-clockwise from the top)
   a crosse – lacrosse
   a *cesta* or basket – jai alai/pelota
   bails – cricket
   a shuttlecock – badminton
   a mitt – baseball

Extension activity

Students can be given a list of sports and asked to discuss what would be the top 10 sports for men and women in their country. Here are the top 10 participation sports in Britain:

Men	Women
1 snooker/pool	1 swimming
2 darts	2 aerobics
3 swimming	3 cycling
4 football	4 snooker/pool
cycling	5 darts
6 jogging	6 jogging
7 golf	badminton
weight training	8 weight training
9 aerobics	9 bowls
10 fishing	equestrian sports
badminton	golf
squash	ice skating
table tennis	netball
	squash
	tennis

Listening technique: specific information

1 Students listen to two students practising for Phase B of the Listening exam and decide if Student B chooses the photograph described by Student A.

Answer

Yes, picture 5 is correct.

2 Students now listen to two native speakers doing a similar activity. Speaker A describes one photograph in detail. Speaker B then talks about two things that are similiar and two things that are different in his/her choice of photograph. Students decide which two photographs are being described.

Answers

Picture 6
Picture 2

3 Students note the list of criteria examiners use to grade a candidate's speaking skills:
• Fluency
• Accuracy
• Pronunciation
• Achievement of task
• Interactive communication (involvement or turn taking)

Students listen to the first recording of the two students and grade them using these five criteria.

Exploring language: ways of improving fluency

Students listen again to the two native speakers in Activity 2 above, making note of the marker words and fillers used.

EXAM FOCUS: (Speaking, Phase B) describing a picture

This activity can be organised either in pairs or in groups of three with one student monitoring and checking how well each of the speakers uses marker words and fillers. Insist that students follow the exam procedure, with Student A describing his/her photographs in detail whilst Student B listens and then decides which two pictures were being described. They can then swap roles.

See **Language awareness: questions (2) (page 47)**

PART THREE
Theme parks

Lead-in

Students discuss the types of fairs or theme park rides they've experienced. If any student has a particularly interesting story, encourage them to share it with the class.

Reading technique: skimming

1–2 Tell students they are going to read about Nemesis, a terrifying ride at a famous British theme park. Discuss why the ride is called Nemesis (meaning 'deserved and unavoidable punishment for wrongdoing' as in the expression 'to meet one's nemesis'). Students read the text to discover which points are mentioned by the writer, and put the points in the correct order.

Answers

In order: d, c, a, f, e

Reading technique: scanning

Answers

a Arguably T or F! The text actually says 'not suitable for expectant mothers', which certainly advises pregnant women not to ride on Nemesis, although does not expressly forbid it. Debate this point with stronger students.

b T ('designed with the sole intention of scaring you witless')

c F ('Nemesis is the only thrill-ride in Europe on which you ride on the outside')

d T ('none of this, it seems, was quite enough')

e T ('legs trembling')

Reading technique: appreciating the writer's tone

1 This activity encourages an appreciation of the writer's tone which is often gently ironic. Students need to be able to determine when the writer is not being entirely serious.

Answers

a H/I

b S/F

c S/F

d H/I

e S/F

f H/I (here the writer is certainly exaggerating for humorous effect)

g H/I

2 Here the students are asked to respond to the writer's description of Nemesis. Conduct a quick survey to determine who would ride on Nemesis given the opportunity.

See **Language awareness: future forms (page 49)**

Exploring language: punctuation marks

At this level students will have a fairly good grasp of the use of punctuation in pieces of formal writing, but may be less confident about exploiting punctuation to create an informal style. This activity should act primarily as revision, although students may be uncertain of the correct pronunciation of some of the terms.

Answers

Punctuation mark	Name	Use(s)
,	apostrophe	1, 5
:	colon	2, 6
-	hyphen	4
' '	quotation marks	3
—	dash	8
( )	brackets	7

Students should be able to find examples of all of these in the text.

EXAM FOCUS: (Writing, Section A)

One of the key skills in this type of exam question is the selection of material relevant for the answer. In addition, there should be a significant difference in terms of register between the letter of complaint (formal) and the letter to a close friend (informal).

Useful phrases for the letter of complaint
- Dear Sir/Madam
- I'm writing to express my disappointment at …
- Although I was impressed by …, I must admit to being dissatisfied by … (language of concession is also useful here to express complaints politely)
- I would suggest that in the future …
- Yours faithfully

Useful phrases for the letter to a friend
- Hi/Dear …/Hello.
- You wouldn't believe the day we had! (Views can be expressed much more directly here)
- With love/Best wishes

Students can work in pairs or groups to plan their letters. Encourage them to write first drafts during the lesson which they can exchange with each other to offer criticism and guidance. They can write final drafts for homework.

LANGUAGE AWARENESS: questions (2)

1–2 Students supply what they think are the correct question tags for each of the sentences a–k. They then listen to the recording and check their answers. Most sentences serve as revision of basic question tags and should not prove too demanding. However, students may encounter difficulties with imperatives.

Answers

a The shop opens at 9.00, doesn't it?

b It's your turn, isn't it?

c Close the door behind you, will/would/can/could you?

d Don't be late, will you?

e Nobody called me, did they?

f You couldn't do me a favour, could you?

g I'm next, aren't I?

h Make sure you're home by 11.00, won't you?

i Give me a hand, will/would/can/could you?

j Everywhere's closed now, isn't it?

k You haven't got the time, have you?

3 Students read the extract and examine the form of question tags when used as imperatives.

Answers

Question tags that follow imperatives differ from the general rule. These tags usually contain modal verbs like 'will/would', 'can/could', depending on whether the statement is an order or a request.

When the imperative is a request, the tag is often positive.

After a negative imperative we generally use 'will you'.

4 Students listen to the recording a second time and mark in the intonation pattern on each of the sentences a–k.

Answers

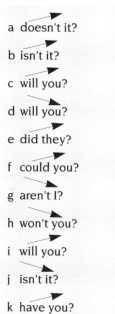

a doesn't it?

b isn't it?

c will you?

d will you?

e did they?

f could you?

g aren't I?

h won't you?

i will you?

j isn't it?

k have you?

5 Having highlighted the correct form and intonation, students now match each sentence to the correct function.

Answers

	A	B
question	a, b, e	
confirmation	g, j	
request	c, f, i, k	
polite order	d, h	

6 Students complete the dialogue with an appropriate question tag. In some cases more than one answer is possible.

Answers

a haven't we?
b will/can you? ('would' or 'could' might be regarded as too polite for the situation)
c will you?
d haven't I?
e have you?
f isn't it?
g can't I?
h didn't you?
i did we?
j isn't she?
k will you?
l aren't I?
m will you?

7 Students now practise the conversation in groups, paying particular attention to intonation. They can then compare their performance with the conversation on tape.

Answers

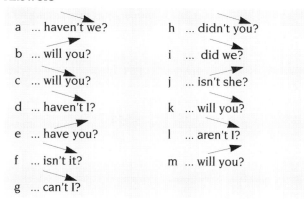

a ... haven't we?   h ... didn't you?

b ... will you?   i ... did we?

c ... will you?   j ... isn't she?

d ... haven't I?   k ... will you?

e ... have you?   l ... aren't I?

f ... isn't it?   m ... will you?

g ... can't I?

8 This activity, adapted from Leo Jones, *English in Use*, gives students the opportunity to practise question tags and demands that they use the correct intonation. Students work in groups of three or four, each person being asked the same five questions.

E.g. When's your birthday?
        Where did you last go on holiday?

When all the questions have been answered by every member of the group, students take it in turns to try to remember information about different colleagues. If they are sure they're correct they use a falling intonation, if they aren't sure they use a rising intonation.

E.g. Your birthday's on the 5th May, isn't it?
        Your last holiday was in Spain, wasn't it?

Point out that question tags, like reply questions examined in Unit 2, are extremely useful in making a conversation interactive, and will be useful in Section C of the speaking paper.

LANGUAGE AWARENESS: future forms

1 Students read the dialogue and underline all the examples of future forms.

A So, <u>it's</u> your birthday on Friday, <u>is it</u>?
B Yeah ... <u>I'll be</u> 21.
A Well, that calls for a celebration. <u>I'm not doing</u> anything then so ....
B Hang on. My <u>girlfriend's coming round</u> in the evening. <u>I'm cooking</u> her a meal.
A Very nice! So <u>you're not going to celebrate</u> your birthday with your mates then?
B Of course <u>I am</u>! <u>She'll probably leave</u> about 9.00 so <u>I'll be</u> free after that.
A OK. What time <u>shall we meet</u>? (*Point out that 'will' could not be used here.*)
B Well, my train <u>gets in</u> at 9.30. <u>Is that</u> too late for you?
A No. There's some things <u>I need</u> to do in the office on Friday, so <u>I'm going to stay</u> till late anyway. <u>I'll meet</u> you at the station. <u>We can</u> try that new restaurant in town.
B Saturday night though, <u>it's going to be</u> busy, <u>isn't it</u>?
A No problem. <u>I'll phone</u> and <u>book</u> a table.
B Great! Dave <u>comes back</u> from his holiday on Friday so <u>I'll give</u> him a ring too.
A OK. <u>See you</u> Friday.

2 Students find examples of the eight functions in the dialogue.

Answers

a **Simple prediction**
She'll probably leave; I'll be free

b **Planned intention**
you're not going to celebrate
I'm going to stay

c **Arrangement**
I'm not doing anything then
My girlfriend's coming round; I'm cooking her a meal

d **Future fact**
I'll be 21

e **Firm prediction**
it's going to be busy

f **Requesting information or decisions about the future**
What time shall we meet?

g **Timetable or calender event**
It's your birthday on Friday, is it?
my train gets in at 9.30
Dave comes back from his holiday

h **Spontaneous decision**
I'll meet you at the station
I'll phone and book a table
I'll give him a ring too

3–4 Having read the information from the authors, which highlights the use of future continuous, future perfect and future perfect continuous, students match each sentence with the appropriate time line.

Answers

Time line 1: c and f
Time line 2: a and d
Time line 3: b and e

5 Students now write sentences about themselves, friends or relatives, using the same structures.

6 This final exercise practises all the future forms featured in the Language Awareness. Students underline the correct form in each of the sentences a–l. Sometimes more than one answer is correct. However, insist that students justify their particular choice.

Answers

a You look exhausted! Sit down. I'll do (<u>spontaneous decision</u>) the washing up.
b I've made an appointment with the dentist. I'm seeing (<u>arrangement</u>) her tomorrow.
c I feel dizzy. I think I'm going to faint. (<u>firm prediction</u>)
d Trains to London leave (<u>timetable</u>) from platform 2.
e I've had enough of this cough! I'm going to (<u>planned intention</u>) give up smoking.
f By the time she takes her exam, she'll have been studying English for six years.
g I hope I'll be feeling confident on the day of the exam.
h You can have the tape later. I'll have listened to it by then.
i I'll see you later (<u>spontaneous decision and a common expression</u>). What time shall we meet?
j I'll have read the book by the time we leave.
k You'll like it in Spain (<u>prediction</u>). The weather's beautiful.
l Don't phone him at six. He'll be eating his dinner.

Human Relationships

PART ONE
An ideal family? (SB page 98)

Lead-in

1 Although the questionnaire is meant as an introduction to the English in Use exercise, ample time should be allowed for discussion should personal or cultural values prove to be varied.

Extension activity
An alternative method of exploiting this questionnaire would be to ask students to modify the statements so that they can agree with them.

E.g. Parents should not be able to enter their child's bedroom unless they suspect he/she is taking drugs/stealing.

Students can then share their ideas in groups or with the whole class.

2 Students read the statements and calculate their score, then compare them. Allow time to discuss statements that prove controversial. Students share views on the points in the rubric. In a mixed-nationality group the various cultural values should be exploited. This could be extended to include a discussion on how teenage demands conflict with parental responsibilities.

EXAM FOCUS: (English in Use Section C) discourse cloze

1 Remind students to read the cloze for general understanding only and not to write anything at this stage.

2 Students listen to Claire and write down her suggestons in the gaps marked 'a' . Students compare answers and listen again if necessary.

The class should discuss the skills Claire used to complete the cloze. Some of these skills include:

- awareness of synonyms and dependent prepositions

  E.g. 'protect/shield', 'to cope with/to face' 'protect from', 'desire to', 'allowed to'

- awareness of sentence construction

  E.g. 'this is going to be a kind of exaggeration of "protecting"' 'now we've got a list of situations here' 'this will be another example'

- awareness of anaphoric reference (referring back):

  E.g. 'now this is referring back to these difficulties'

Answers
Claire's choices:
1a from difficulties
2a restricting a child's every movement
3a to shield the child
4a to sort problems out
5a to face disappointments
6a such problems
7a and independent
8a feeling loved perhaps
9a This is not a good thing

3
Answers
1b E
2b L
3b A
4b G
5b K
6b C
7b J
8b H
9b B

Writing skill: a magazine article

This is a structured writing task with the word limit the same as for the CAE exam. Point out the difference between a straightforward FCE type 'advantages and disadvantages' essay, which examines one topic, and a contrast and comparison essay, which compares two or more topics.

1 Hold a quick class survey to discover the average number of brothers and/or sisters that students have. Find out if there are any students who are the only child in their family. Ascertain what some of the advantages and disadvantages are from both perspectives.

2 Students complete the table with as many pros and cons as they can think of. There is no need for them to be in any order at this stage.

3 Students now organise their random points into possible paragraphs topics. Explain that lines should be drawn connecting any related points. When this is done, students give each category a title.

4 Students complete the cloze exercise. They should be encouraged to discuss the fact that, although grammatically more than one choice exists, for purposes of coherence the choices are limited.

Answers

On the one hand
In contrast
However
on the contrary

5 Students will no doubt be very well acquainted with such connecting words, having spent many writing lessons examining their uses. Unfortunately, it is quite often the case that students use these words or expressions unnecessarily if, for example, their meaning is already conveyed in the context of the text. The result is that their writing can appear unnatural. Ask students to read through the passage again and decide which of the connecting words or expressions could be omitted without affecting meaning.

Answer

'On the one hand' could be omitted without meaning or clarity being affected.

6 Students now write the competition entry, concentrating on their use (and non-use) of connecting words. A follow-up activity could include students marking each other's work, paying attention to organisation and cohesion.

PART TWO
Family conflicts

Lead-in
During this lead-in activity, students are asked to think of the types of issues that married couples argue about.

Photo 1
Possible topics include:
- the relationship (jealousy of previous partners, infidelity)
- children (whether or not to have them, how many children to have, naming children)
- money (what spending priorities should be)

Photo 2
Students will probably have fewer ideas, because time tends to heal differences!

Reading technique: skimming

Try not to let students spend more than three minutes on this activity. Ask them how they might best read the text quickly whilst at the same time finding the main points: they could suggest reading the first and perhaps the second sentence in each paragraph, or the opening and closing sentences.

Answer

Since Tom has retired from work, Helen has become increasingly irritated at Tom's interference in household matters.

Vocabulary development: describing personal characteristics

This activity is designed to test students' knowledge of these common adjectives. If they are not familiar with any of the words they should be encouraged to use their dictionaries (English–English). They are also required to justify their decisions by:

a referring directly to the text for evidence
b using their skills of inference (i.e. reading between the lines).

Extension activity
In groups of three, students can role-play a meeting between Tom, Helen and a counsellor. Following the meetings the groups can report to the class the decisions that were reached.

Writing skill: a report for a magazine

This is a structured writing task, with the word limit the same as for the CAE exam. The first task (writing the notes from the point of view of the counsellor) focuses the students' note taking and is designed to give practice in summary writing.

Encourage the students to brainstorm for writing ideas together and then follow the instructions for writing their report. This is also an ideal opportunity to encourage peer group correction of earlier drafts. As we suggested earlier, students could work together as editors of the magazine in which the problem page reply is to be published, their role being to choose the best reply for publication. There is a sample student answer on page 149 of the student's Book.

PART THREE
The colours of love (SB page 103)

Lead-in

1–2 Students read the quotes and discuss which of the statements agrees most with their idea of 'love'. The four statements offer different perspectives on how being in love makes you feel, so this is a good opportunity to consolidate vocabulary describing emotions.

Reading technique: prediction

1–3 It is not expected that students will be able to think of all six categories of love dealt with in the article. Students read the categories, checking their predictions and deciding which of the categories most applies to them. Any feedback session should be sensitive to the fact that students might not wish to discuss their own emotions. Ask them which category best describes them or their (ideal) partner.

Reading technique: comprehension

Students should be encouraged to use skimming skills in order to match the statements with the appropriate definition, underlining key words in both sections of the text.

Answers

A 4 (key words: attracted, physical chemistry, emotionally involved; passionate, intimate)

B 6 (key words: uncertain ... commitments, keep secret, other partners; game, wary of, cynical)

C 2 (key words: friendship, caring, deep; solid, down to earth, enduring)

D 5 (key words: serious, background, parent, career, family; logically, shopping list)

E 3 (key words: stomach ... upset, killing myself, stupid things, attention, possessive, dependent, low self-esteem)

F 1 (Key words: help, sacrifice; all-giving, selfless, non-demanding, kind)

See **Language awareness: conditionals (page 10)**

Vocabulary development: emotions

Students are required to sort the words into categories of similar meaning. They may need guidance from you in explaining the various shades of meaning between words in the same category, if they don't possess a good dictionary.

Answers

dislike, hate, disgust
irritation, anger, rage
tranquillity, contentment, serenity, calm
fear, horror, terror
infatuation, love, adoration
sadness, sorrow, grief

Students should choose three or four of the nouns that describe particular experiences in the last five years of their lives. It might help to get the ball rolling if you give a few examples from your own past – the more personal the experience the better. When students are ready they should discuss their memories in groups.

Listening technique: global understanding

1 Students listen to the tape of the speaker reading out the letter. Allow cross-checking.

Answers

Romantic meal	5
Party	2
Athens airport	3
UK airport	6
Meeting at university	4
Indian meal	1

Listening technique: specific information

Students listen again, but this time paying attention to the use of tenses and ordering the pictures chronologically.

Answers

Meeting at university	1
Party	2
Indian meal	3
Athens airport	4
Romantic meal	5
UK airport	6

See **Language awareness: past tense forms (page 54)**

See **Language awareness: past tense forms (page 54)**

EXAM FOCUS: ((Speaking, Phase B) information gap

In this activity Student A is required to speak for one minute before Student B starts talking. Once this first stage is complete, if all the differences have not been found students can then start questioning each other. Organise the students into pairs. If there are odd numbers, have two students working together or have somebody monitoring pairs for feedback later. Insist that students sit opposite each other and do not let their partner see their picture. Students will have to describe their picture in detail if they are to find all the differences.

Answers

The main differences are:

Student A:
Man offering woman food
Man not wearing glasses
Man and woman looking at each other
Food on table
Waiter has his back to them
One person visible behind

Student B:
Man holding menu
Man wearing glasses
Man looking at waiter
No food on table
Waiter is at their table
Two or three people visible behind

LANGUAGE AWARENESS: conditionals

1   Students examine the eight sentences from the article 'The Colours of Love'. Students often narrowly define conditionals as sentences containing 'will' and 'if'. This exercise is intended to reinforce the function of these structures and to show that varying degrees of reality can be expressed by means of various forms. Hold a feedback session when students have examined the sentences and highlight the following:

2   'Were I to win' (instead of 'If I won')
3   'provided'
4   'probably'
6   'unless'
7   'might not have chosen'

2–3   Students categorise the sentences in terms of 'real' and 'unreal' situations. The four categories represent the basic types of conditional sentences; zero, first, second and third.

Answers

Zero:	5, 8
First:	3, 6
Second:	1, 2
Third:	4, 7

4   These four sentences introduce the notion of 'mixed conditionals'. Students should have no trouble identifying this and should be encouraged to explain the use of these structures before looking at the Grammar Reference.

5   Students decide on the most appropriate conditionals and complete the dialogue.

Answers

a   wouldn't have rushed
b   had known
c   had taken
d   could/would be sitting
e   hurry
f   will miss
g   knew
h   had had
i   might/ would be
j   don't stop
k   will miss
l   will get
m   buy
n   had told
o   could/would have brought
p   could

Extension activity

Students can think of some major turning points in their lives so far. They then express how their lives changed or didn't change, using third or mixed conditionals.

E.g. If I hadn't gone to university, I'd never have met Tony.
If I had stayed in my previous job, I'd almost certainly be unemployed now.

LANGUAGE AWARENESS: past tense forms

1–2 Having read the short extract, students match the circled verbs with the corrrect definitions.

Answers

had been	action in an earlier past
stopped	one of a sequence of completed actions in the past
greeted	one of a sequence of completed actions in the past
made	one of a sequence of completed actions in the past
'd been thinking	activity in progress or repeated action in an earlier past
was shaking	a past action in progress at the same time as another
Was he blushing	a past action in progress at the same time as another
had carried	action in an earlier past
was looking	an action in progress in the past
was preparing/heard	a long action or event in the past interrupted by a shorter action or event
would	future in the past

3 Students look for other examples of these uses in the story.

4 Visual representations of tense usage, such as time lines, can often enhance comprehension. This activity asks students to create time lines for the circled verbs in the previous activity. There are no 'correct' answers here, but the representation should show clearly the use of the particular tense. The following time lines serve as examples.

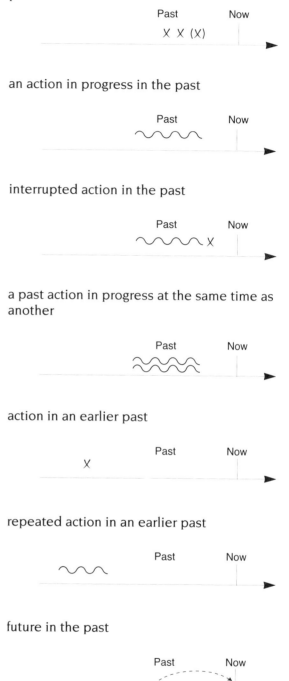

one of a sequence of completed actions in the past

an action in progress in the past

interrupted action in the past

a past action in progress at the same time as another

action in an earlier past

repeated action in an earlier past

future in the past

5 Students turn to the tapescript on page 163, look again at the letter and try to supply the correct tenses. Allow time for students to discuss their ideas before playing the tape.

Answers

a	went
b	left
c	was sitting/sat
d	had seen
e	hadn't been able to
f	arrived/had arrived
g	came
h	had left
i	had been writing
j	had invited
k	came
l	spent
m	plucked
n	had felt
o	met/had met
p	had felt
q	had spent
r	flew
s	met
t	had been delayed
u	arrived
v	had been waiting

6–7 This activity, adapted from *Grammar* by Rob Batstone (Oxford University Press), highlights how past and past modal forms are often used to create 'distance'. This can be in terms of hypothetical distance, social distance, temporal distance, and distance in terms of what is believed to be true. Students read the four groups of sentences and match each group with the appropriate category.

Answers

First group:	hypothetical distance
Second group:	social distance
Third group:	temporal distance
Fourth group:	what is believed to be true (c is seen as most true)

Extension activity

A great way to practise past tenses (and great fun too) is the Alibi Game. Tell the students that the previous night the police found somebody lying dead outside the school. The person had been murdered and the police believe the murderer was one of the students. You don't believe this for one minute and have decided to help the students invent an alibi, a description of their whereabouts which would make it impossible for them to have been anywhere near the school at the time of the murder.

Students must work in pairs and pretend that they were together all evening. They should decide what they did, where they went, what they were wearing, etc. Having worked out their story, one pair is then interviewed by the class. One student leaves the room while his/her partner is questioned for two or three minutes. Nominate a secretary who should make notes of the student's answers. When the time is up the first student leaves the room and the second student is then asked exactly the same questions. Each time the answer differs, the pair are given one point. At the end of the session the pair with the most points are the murderers.

This is an extremely popular activity and students quickly forget the object of the exercise; namely to practise past tenses. Correction can be carried out by the teacher immediately, although this tends to disrupt the activity. Alternatively, the student being questioned can refuse to answer any questions he/she feels are grammatically incorrect.

The World of Work

PART ONE
Work values (SB page 109)

Lead-in

1 This activity acts as a lead-in to the profile of Danny Price, a choreographer/dancer, but can be planned as an extended speaking activity depending on time available. Start by finding out what the students' attitude to work is. If the group are predominantly employed, students can be asked if they feel they are well suited to their job, the reasons they chose it, whether they 'live to work' or 'work to live'. Students who have not yet started work can be asked similar questions, but questions about their future ambitions or choice of career should be avoided as this will interfere with Activity 2.

Students check the meanings of the six idioms and decide which best describes their attitude towards work. In groups, they discuss their choices and their reasons for making them.

2 Students work in small groups. The activity can be carried out in either of these two ways:

- Individual students look through the list of values and decide which ones apply to them. When each member of the group is ready, students can try to guess what the work values of their colleagues might be. One student in each group should act as secretary, making notes on each person.
- Alternatively students have a general discussion on their work values, again with one person taking notes.

3 Still in groups but working alone, students think of two or three ideal jobs for each member of the group, based on the profile drawn up in Activity 2. They then share their ideas with the group and find out who would be the best careers adviser.

Extension activity
The activity can be developed somewhat with the inclusion of some authentic job advertisements. A wide selection of occupations should be included and given to each group. Following the discussion on work values, students, acting as careers advisers, can offer appropriate jobs to each of their colleagues. An obvious follow-up activity would be for students to write a letter of application, perhaps including a separate CV.

Listening technique: specific information

1 Students read the profile of Danny Price to get an idea of the subject matter. When they have finished, allow them a few minutes to discuss in pairs what they think the missing information could be, ideas which can then be shared as a class. This will give students a greater sense of purpose in listening to the interview and also help them to focus on relevant information needed to complete this activity which mirrors Section A and C of the listening paper.

Answers

1 acting/drama
2 six hours
3 gets faster
4 little solos
5 chorus dancer
6 West End musical
7 three brothers
8 a princess
9 a fish called
10 having any money
11 the world
12 23 countries
13 equality and racism

2 Allow students to listen for a second time if necessary and to share their ideas in pairs before they give their answers. Explain that they should pay attention to spelling as well as content.

3 In pairs or groups, students discuss which of the work values listed in the lead-in activity would seem to apply to a career in dance. Is this a profession that appeals to any of them?

Vocabulary development: some common expressions

1 This is a brief exercise to exploit some of the vocabulary from the listening. Students rewrite the words and expressions to show that they understand their meaning. You could also point out that 'wise', as in 'diet-wise', is a useful suffix to remember as it is often used in informal English meaning 'concerning the subject of ...'.

   E.g. Food-wise he tends to avoid eating red meat.

2 This is another activity which highlights the importance of the schwa sound in English, and in particular the number of vowel sounds that can become schwa in connected speech. The schwa sounds that are always contained in the words are:

   you can pig out on past<u>a</u>   /pastə/

   vic<u>iou</u>s cir<u>cle</u>   /ə/ /vɪʃəs/ /sɜːkəl/

   Those that become schwas in connected speech are:

   <u>you can</u> pig out on pasta   /jə kən/

   like <u>a</u> household name   /ə/

   here's <u>a</u> cocktail   /ə/

   into <u>a</u> vicious circle   /ə/

EXAM FOCUS: (Writing, Section A)

1 Students underline exactly what the task is in the instructions and then compare their ideas with a partner. The important information is that it is a letter to a friend, and is therefore informal, and that this friend wants information about the college and any advice the student might be able to offer. Students should also note that a degree of invention is allowed but that they must not alter any of the information given.

2 Students should then do the same with the letter, underlining all the points that need to be answered. These should include most of the following.

   She wants some information about:
   • a good dance college in London if possible
   • the cost and length of the course
   • clothes needed
   • the qualifications required.

It is also important to note that she does have some experience in dance which the prospectus asks for and which could therefore be included in the letter.

3 Students now search the prospectus and the magazine article for the necessary information. When they feel they have sufficient information to write their letter, some time can be spent discussing how they could begin and end this letter. Some comment could be made about Debbie's holiday, for example, and maybe there should be some short snippets of information from the writer before starting the main body of the letter.

4 Students shouldn't have any difficulty identifying the need for informality, and will no doubt be aware of the layout of informal letters, although this could be dealt with in terms of revision.

Extension activity
Ask students to refer back to Unit 5 where formal and informal structures are covered in detail. They can check and, if necessary, correct or rewrite their work with reference to the points which come up there.

There is a sample student answer on page 152 of the Student's Book.

PART TWO
Finding the right person for the job
(SB page 112)

Lead-in

1 This lead-in elicits students' opinions on the issue of using graphology as a recruitment tool. If your students are particularly sceptical you can remind them that in France, for example, handwriting analysis is used commonly in companies looking for new employees. The questions are intended to be light-hearted, and not necessarily convincing!

Answers
   a A
   b A
   c B

2 Conduct a class discussion on the validity of using handwriting analysis in this way. Write other examples on the board (e.g., interviews, trade tests, psychometric tests) and ask students to give each one marks out of 10 for their effectiveness.

EXAM FOCUS: (English in Use, Section A) lexical cloze and open cloze

This section provides practice in both the clozes in Section A of this paper, namely the lexical cloze (question 1) and the open cloze (question 2). Before starting, ask the students to read the instructions for both tasks on page 114. Students work in pairs, with each one completing one of the tests and then sharing opinions with their partner. Alternatively, you could have everybody working on cloze A in one group (sharing answers) and cloze B likewise. The questions in Activity 2 require the students to reflect on what type of knowledge they need to complete their cloze type.

Answers

A

1 applicant
2 undertake
3 evaluating
4 practical
5 incapable
6 in-built
7 aptitude
8 high-level
9 accepted
10 validity

B

1 may/could/might
2 is
3 in/for
4 into
5 All
6 be
7 for
8 with
9 most
10 two/results

In a final feedback session, you should have elicited the following information about each question type.

- **Open cloze:** Missing items are usually grammatical words, e.g. prepositions, quantifiers, auxiliary verbs.

- Lexical cloze: missing items are content words, e.g. nouns, main verbs, adjectives.

The main focus in a lexical cloze is on choosing the correct lexical collocation for each space (not always easy!) as well as exercising a certain amount of grammatical knowledge (e.g. to be incapable of doing something). A useful technique to help students understand and actively improve their ability to find adjective–noun collocations is to encourage them to learn phrases or chunks of language (e.g. 'high-level jobs', 'in-built characteristics').

Listening technique: specific information

1 This question leads in to the topic of the listening texts by asking the students to recall any funny or disastrous experiences they have already had. You can also take part in this activity, as students are always keen to hear personal anecdotes from their teachers!

2 Students listen to the tape in order to tick off each of the points listed. Encourage them to try and understand the context of each point. They should make notes and listen again as necessary.

3 This activity focuses on grammatical accuracy (see a similar activity in Unit 2, page 26). It can take students quite a long time to complete, so we recommend that pairs work together or divide the questions between them.

Suggested answers

a What job had he given up?
b Why did he like the idea of being a milkman?
c How many questions were on the test?
d What answer did he give to the question about how many weeks' holidays he would like to have a year?
e What did the man find when he compared the two graphs?
f What answer did he give to the question of what time he wanted to get up in the mornings?
g How did he feel about the test?

4 You can end this section with a final discussion on finding the right person for the job.

See **Language awareness: verb forms (2) (page 60)**

PART THREE
Trade unions (SB page 115)

Lead-in

1–2 Students read through the eight statements on trade unions and give each a score from one to five. Working in groups, they then hold a discussion, putting forward their opinions and trying, ultimately, to get students with different opinions to change their scores.

EXAM FOCUS: (Reading) multiple matching

Students read the article, 'A New Deal for Youth' and complete the multiple matching activity. Try to encourage students to finish this activity in 20 minutes with a further five minutes allowed for them to check their answers in pairs.

Answers

1	E
2	A
3	D
4	G
5	B
6	C
7	E
8	A and C
9	A
10	E, F and G
11	D, F and G

See **Language awareness: participles (2) (page 61)**

EXAM FOCUS: (English in Use, Section C) expanded notes

1 Students work in pairs and decide which kind of words or structures are required to turn the notes into sentences. Defining and non-defining relative clauses are very common in this exercise, as are dependent prepositions and appropriate linking words. Attention must also be paid to tenses and verb forms.

2 Once students are aware of the necessary structures, they can work alone or in pairs, expanding the notes into full sentences.

3 Students finally check the meanings of the sentences they have created in the context of the leaflet generally.

Suggested answers

1 The company is concerned at this turn of events and believes it is necessary to explain the situation so that you make the correct decision.

2 Although company profits were up last year, strike action would be very damaging and would threaten productivity.

3 Competition in this industry, which has suffered through economic recession, has never been fiercer.

4 Your trade union, which has refused to enter (into) negotiations, is acting irresponsibly by asking you to strike.

5 If the strike goes ahead we must warn you that redundancies will happen.

6 We must remind you that the company's 5% offer, which is above the national average, is final.

7 As we move into the 21st century, trade unions must realise that there is a need for more responsible behaviour.

8 The company hopes that the employees will understand the seriousness of the situation and refuse to take strike action.

Extension activity

To give students further practice in this type of activity the teacher can read out a text at normal speed. This should be about the same length as a fully expanded Section C text. The students should make brief notes and if necessary listen a second time. They can then try to expand their notes into full sentences. Suitable texts include factual descriptions of people or places often found in encyclopedias.

Vocabulary development: common abbreviations

1 In pairs, students write the abbreviations in full.

Answers

a	Re	Regarding
b	PTO	Please turn over
c	Enc.	Enclosed
d	cc	copy circulated
e	req.	required
	50 k	50,000

2 Students discuss the meaning of the abbreviations and the context in which they would be found.

Answers

1 ad – advertisement (conversation)
2 hols – holidays, V. – Very, Fave – Favourite, esp. – especially (message on a postcard)
3 accom. – accommodation, pw – per week, pref. – preferred (advertisement)
4 (p+p inc) – postage and packing included (advertisement)
5 etc. – etcetera (notice)
6 Cap. – Capital, Pop. 6m approx. – Population 6 million approximately (travel guide)
7 10m – 10 metres (notice)
8 pp. – pages, ch. – chapter (college or university reading instructions)

LANGUAGE AWARENESS: verb forms (2)

1 Ask students to underline all the examples of 'to' + infinitive in the eight sentences. When they have highlighted the forms they match each one to the appropriate heading.

Answers

a to show purpose
b to show purpose
c after certain verbs
d after the object of certain verbs
e as the subject of a sentence
f as the subject of a sentence
g after most adjectives
h after most adjectives

2 Individually or in pairs, students convert the notes into full sentences using appropriate infinitive constructions. Point out that this activity is similar to the exercise in Section C of the English in Use paper in which knowledge of verb forms is often being tested. Students will also need to concentrate on prepositions and tenses.

Answers

a It was great to receive your last letter.
b This is just a short note to tell you about my recent holiday.
c My friends persuaded/had persuaded me to go on holiday to England.
d I'd never been to England before and I was determined to have a good time.
e On the first day we went to London to see the sights.

f Unfortunately, I didn't remember to take an umbrella. It rained all day.
g Still, it was interesting to see all the famous buildings.

3 This activity highlights the way different verb forms can lead to a change in meaning with certain words. Students read the two example sentences for each verb form then, individually or in pairs, complete the third example with the correct verb form.

Answers

a remember + gerund: connected to the past, a memory
b remember + to + infinitve: remember something that has to be done
c You were sleep-walking last night. Do you remember walking into my bedroom?

a forget + gerund: connected to the past, to forget something that happened
b forget + to + infinitive: forget something that has to be done
c I forgot to pay the gas bill. Do you think they'll cut us off?

a stop + to + infinitive: stop doing something (maybe temporarily) in order to do something else
b stop + gerund: stop doing something
c Can we stop arguing all the time? Let's be friends!

a go on + to + infinitive: to move on to doing something after something else
b go on + gerund: to continue doing something that has been started
c She was so lazy! Her tutors never realised she would go on to become famous.

4 This is an opportunity for students to revise verb forms with a reply to the letter that appeared in Activity 2. Students read the letter and correct all the mistakes they can find.

Answers

I was sorry to hear
remember to take
to avoid the sun
I'd rather lie on the beach
and visit boring old buildings
to pass my English exam
suggested that I try CAE
I'd better finish
She doesn't even allow students to finish

I must go
I enjoy reading
it would be nice to talk
I hope to hear

5 This final activity gives students the chance to practise the verb forms covered in this section. Encourage them to complete the task orally. You can start by giving an example yourself to show the students what is required.

LANGUAGE AWARENESS:
participles (2)

1 Students read the article for general understanding, explaining the headline 'Tests in the Dock'.

Answer

Psychometric tests are on trial (the accused in a court case stands in the dock).

2 Students find and underline all the examples of present and past participles used like reduced relative clauses, and then write them out as full relatiive clauses. The basic distinction between progressive and past participles is whether the meaning is active or passive. However, when converting the reduced relative clauses into full relative clauses, students will notice that the choice of tense is not always straightforward. Encourage them to consider the context and to decide from this which form is most appropriate.

Answers

- Tests used by companies
- Tests that/which are used by companies
- companies turning to psychometric tests
- companies that/which are turning to psycho-metric tests
- reservations expressed during the 1980s
- reservations that/which were expressed during the 1980s
- People attending interviews
- People who have attended interviews
- they now face questionnaires concealing investigations
- they now face questionnaires that/which conceal/are concealing investigations
- psychologists argue that tests compiled and analysed incorrectly
- psychologists argue that tests that/which are/have been compiled and analysed incorrectly

3 Individually or in pairs, students decide which verb is appropriate for each pair of sentences and whether the past or the present participle should be used in each.

Answers

a 1 Any luggage left unattended will be removed by the police.
  2 Employees leaving the premises should ensure all lights are extinguished.

b 1 People buying duty-free goods must show their boarding passes.
  2 Goods bought during the sale cannot be returned.

c 1 Plants grown under artificial light tend to grow much quicker.
  2 Gardeners growing sensitive plants should beware of an early frost this year.

d 1 Students taking examinations should report to Room 101.
  2 Photographs taken within the restricted area were confiscated by officials.

e 1 Anyone damaging company property will be dismissed.
  2 Buildings damaged by the storm may have to be demolished.

4 Point out that participles can often be used to express various meanings in formal contexts. Students match the meanings to the five sentences.

Answers

a with the result
b when
c if this is done
d after
e because

5–6 Students practise turning informal sentences into more formal equivalents using participles. If students are coping quite well with these structures, they can attempt Activity 6 at the same time, converting the phrasal verbs into formal equivalents. If this is likely to prove distracting, do the activities in two stages.

Answers

a Having arrived late, he missed the flight.
b Taken regularly, the tablets should cure the infection.
c Arriving at the ground, he realised the game had been cancelled.

d The government abolished state pensions,
  leaving many people penniless.
e Having left university, he entered the legal
  profession.

Encourage students to make a note of these formal
structures on page 147 of the Student's Book.

Power Relationships

PART ONE
At the top (SB page 121)

Lead-in

This activity introduces the article from *The Guardian* on assassination. Avoid talking about the subject before the students have attempted the lead-in activity, as this would destroy the object of the exercise. A competitive element can be incorporated into this activity. Working together in teams, students should collect as much information as they can on the four people as well as choosing the odd one out.

Answers

The odd one out is the assassin, Illich Ramirez Sanchez, or Carlos the Jackal (bottom right). Born in Venezuela, he carried out several kidnappings and other outrages. He gained his name from the film *The Day of the Jackal* as well as a false name he once used on a passport, Carlos Martinez. The others (all victims of assassination) are:

- Reverend Doctor Martin Luther King (top left). Assassinated in Memphis on April 4th 1968. Leader of the American Civil Rights movement, he was killed by James Earl Ray, a white man opposed to equal rights for black people.
- Indira Gandhi. Assassinated in Delhi on October 31st 1984. She was killed by two Sikh bodyguards after ordering her troops to an occupation by separatist Sikhs of the Golden Temple, their holiest site. Later, her son Rajiv, was blown up by Tamil separatists.
- Archduke Franz Ferdinand of Austria, heir to the Austrian throne. Assassinated in Sarajevo on June 28th 1914 by a Bosnian Serb angered by Austria's earlier annexation of Bosnia-Herzegovina. The assassination triggered the start of the First World War.

Ask students if they know of any other political leaders who have shared the same fate. In a multi-cultural group where students have other examples from their own country, they can give an informal presentation on the issues surrounding any (attempted) assassination.

Reading technique: identifying paragraph topics

This reading activity follows exactly the format of the sentence cloze in the exam. However, the activity is not too demanding, as most of the sentences are good examples of topic sentences. Therefore try to encourage students to finish within five minutes. Do not allow students to use a dictionary for this activity.

When they have finished they should compare their answers in groups, highlighting the words or phrases that helped them make their decisions. Avoid giving any answers at this stage, to enable them to justify decisions and if necessary to make their own alterations.

Answers

a 6
b 2
c 7
d 3
e 4
f 9
g 8

Extension activity

Hopefully, whilst discussing how they came to their decisions, students explained how they cross-referenced certain key vocabulary in order to match the topic sentences correctly. It might be useful to point out how reading and writing skills are often transferable. The reading techniques the students used to complete this exercise can be put to good use when writing; for example:

- organising paragraphs around topic sentences
- using synonyms or word substitution to avoid repetition.

Students can practise writing topic sentences by using suitable authentic texts. Photocopy a text containing good examples of topic sentences and delete the opening sentences of each paragraph. Give students copies of the text and ask them, in pairs or groups to read each paragraph. Explain that the idea is not to re-create a sentence as close as possible to the original but simply to produce one which introduces the content of each paragraph. Students can then compare their ideas before seeing the original text. They may find that their own ideas are as good as, if not better than, the original as examples of topic sentences.

1–2 Students compare their answers in groups. The questions require them to read for comprehension (2 and 3), for inference (1), for opinion (4) and for the purpose of the text (5). The Student's Book refers students back to Unit 3 to remind them of how multi-choice questions are often constructed; namely, that there is generally one obviously incorrect answer, two answers that appear correct until closer inspection, and the correct answer. Encourage students to narrow down their choices by rejecting those answers that are obviously incorrect. To avoid simply testing, they should be encouraged to underline evidence in the text for their choices and should be given time to defend these choices in groups before the correct answers are given.

Answers

    1 D
    2 B
    3 D
    4 D
    5 A

3 This topic is clearly controversial and whether the activity is kept on a general level or discussed in relation to current world issues will depend upon the particular group of Students.

See **Language awareness: emphatic structures (page 10)**

Vocabulary development: guessing unknown words

1 It is likely that the meaning of most of these words will be unknown. Do not allow students to use dictionaries until they have made some attempt at guessing the meanings.

2 Discuss the factors that helped students guess the correct meanings. The following will probably be mentioned:

- the position of the word in the sentence which gives clues to the part of speech it is
- logical inference
- students' own world knowledge
- knowledge of similar words

Writing skill: revision of narrative tenses

The picture strip tells the story of Guy Fawkes. Born in Protestant England in 1570, he is famous as the person who tried unsuccessfully to blow up the Houses of Parliament in London. He converted to Roman Catholicism and joined a band of conspirators led by Robert Catesby. After planting up to 20 barrels of gunpowder in cellars under Parliament, the plotters were discovered and Fawkes was arrested. He was found guilty and executed. Each year on November 5th the people of Britain celebrate Guy Fawkes Day. Bonfires are built and effigies of the conspirator are placed at the top.

This writing activity offers practice in narrative tenses and in particular the method of incorporating 'flashback' in story-telling as a means of increasing interest or creating surprise.

1 Students use the past simple and past continuous to tell the story as it appears in the picture strip, (that is, in chronological order), using the vocabulary supplied.

2 Hopefully, students will agree that their stories aren't particularly dramatic. Explain that it is possible to increase the dramatic effect by changing the sequence of events. For example, the story could start at picture 10 where Fawkes is being executed.

'On the 27th January 1606 Fawkes was executed ...'

A beginning of this kind stimulates interest in the reader who immediately has several unanswered questions:

- Who is Fawkes?
- Why was he executed?

However, such a beginning also means that care must be taken with tenses. Events that happened before the execution are therefore 'past in the past'; but, for reasons of style, it wouldn't be appropriate to write all the previous events in the past perfect and/or past continuous. For example, the story could continue:

'Although born a Protestant, Fawkes had converted to Catholicism and went/had gone to The

Netherlands to join the Spanish Army. He became well-known for his bravery...'

The first sentence makes it clear we have travelled back to an earlier past and so further use of the past perfect, although not wrong, is unnecessary. Now ask students to write the story, this time following the sequence below:
Pictures: 4, 1, 2, 3, 5, 10, 6, 7, 8, 9.

3 Students compare stories, commenting on how well events have been linked together and on the use of past tenses.

Extension activity

Students can devise a sequence of their own and write the story for homework. Alternatively, they can write their own life story or relate a personal anecdote. Any of these ideas should first be prepared well, with students listing the main events and then deciding which of these should open the story, remembering that the objective is to create interest or surprise.

PART TWO
Between the sexes (SB page 125)

Lead-in

1–3 Students rate the various adjectives describing men and women on a falling scale from 6 to 1. Make it clear that they should think in terms of stereotypical men and women rather than individual personalities. Having compared opinions, students work in pairs or groups to list suitable antonyms. Stress the importance of collocation here. Adjectives describing personality are required. Consequently, 'guilty' may be the opposite of 'innocent', but this is obviously not suitable.

Answers

These should serve as examples. Students will no doubt think of more.

emotional	unemotional/reserved/cool
aggressive	unassertive/mild-mannered
caring	uncaring/indifferent
sensitive	insensitive/thick-skinned/impenetrable
expressive	taciturn/uncommunicative
talkative	taciturn/uncommunicative/quiet
assertive	unassertive/timid
sentimental	unsentimental/unromantic/level-headed

selfish	unselfish/selfless/altruistic
tender	rough/brutal/aggressive
innocent	worldly/depraved

Speaking skill: sharing opinions

1–2 Give students a few minutes to discuss the question of whether any differences are a consequence of nature or nurture; that is, whether differences are biologically or socially constructed. Obviously care should be taken not to offend students whose cultures clearly designate gender-specific roles. With an appropriate group, the discussion can be expanded to examine how society might influence the behaviour of men and women.

Ask students to form two groups. Group A discuss the different attitudes parents generally have towards boys and girls. They should consider the kind of toys boys and girls are given and the behaviour expected from each. Group B should think about the ways in which men and women are often portrayed, particularly in adverts. Students can then share their opinions as a class.

3 Students should fill in only the first column of the chart outlining gender roles.

4 Having completed the chart for 'Your country', students discuss the various responsibilities and powers that men and women have in their countries. Encourage students to think of justifications for (and, in suitable groups, criticisms of) such gender divisions. Can any of these responsibilities be explained in terms of the points discussed in the previous activities? If necessary, explain 'breadwinner': a person whose earnings support his or her family.

Reading technique: scanning

Students scan the article as quickly as possible to complete the chart. Encourage speed reading by allowing the students two minutes to complete the activity, a task which will be made easier if they search the text for key words like 'proposing', 'education', 'budget' etc. 'Breadwinner' does not appear in the text and students will therefore have to search for an appropriate synonym.

Answers

Proposing marriage	W
Deciding on the children's education	W
Controlling the family budget	W
Inheriting land and property	W
Being the breadwinner	M

Reading technique: inferring meaning

Inference is often an area that causes problems for students, possibly due to the fact that they spend a great deal of time on detail and consequently fail to read between the lines.

Answers

1 This paragraph is in contrast to the information that follows. The women are described as being quite ordinary in appearance and behaviour, yet it is these same women who exercise extraordinary powers in their society.

2 The writer doesn't really give an opinion on whether this is a good or a bad thing.

3 The answer appears to lie in the fact that Trikeri is a matrilocal society. As the man goes to live with the woman when married, it is the woman's family who benefit.

EXAM FOCUS: (English in Use Section A) open cloze

1 Refer students to page 113 for an explanation of the 'open cloze' question. This requires them to supply correct grammatical items.

2 Encourage students to justify their decisions to each other and not to rely on you for answers unless a stalemate is reached.

Answers

a like	f each
b at/for	g too
c well	h with
d nearly/almost	i to
e that	j just/almost

Extension activity

Students can design a clozed text using either a piece of their own written work or a text of their own choosing. Tell them to refer back to page 113 and to note the kind of words that are omitted, namely grammatical words like prepositions, auxiliary or modal verbs, relative pronouns etc. They should then delete a selection of these words from their text and give it to another student to complete.

PART THREE
Campaign groups (SB page 128)

Lead-in

1–3 Ask students if they have ever been involved in a campaign. This doesn't need to be a high-profile political campaign but could include issues that concerned them at school or in the local community, or involved writing a letter to the local paper. Try to get conversation going between those who feel change can be brought by making a stand against the powers that be and those who see it as futile or something that should be avoided. Encourage students to list the kinds of issues that would make them angry or concerned enough to take some form of action.

Reading technique: predicting

Explain the conventions of newspaper headlines in Britain. They are short and to the point, the choice of vocabulary being economical and descriptive. Grammar is usually simplified, prepositions and articles are often left out and tenses are generally limited to the present and past. Are these conventions similar in other countries?

Students imagine the stories that might have accompanied the headlines.

Reading technique: scanning

Students match the headlines with the appropriate story. Encourage speed reading by enforcing the one-minute time limit. Students compare answers.

Answers

1 b
2 c
3 d
4 e
5 a

Listening technique: global understanding

Students read the reports more carefully, and then listen to the radio broadcast to decide how many listeners' letters each story receives. Allow students to compare answers and to listen again if neccessary.

Answers

MOTORWAY STORM	✓
YOUTH CLUB DANGER	✓
WILDLIFE THREAT	✓✓
SUPPORT FOR NURSERIES	✓✓
SHELTER ALERT	✓✓

EXAM FOCUS: (Listening, Section A) gap fill

Students listen to the broadcast again, this time completing the clozed reports. Explain that no more than three words are required. Once again, allow students to compare answers and listen once more if necessary.

Answers

1 the young/young people
2 shop fronts
3 two miles
4 Save Our Village
5 New Youth Club
6 10,000
7 native plants
8 (major) campaign
9 Nurseries for All
10 15,000

Vocabulary development: homophones

1 Students decide on the two meanings of the homophones in the headlines and then imagine the content of the report.

Answers

SUITE SUCCESS   a suite of furniture
                sweet success

The report told of a furniture manufacturer who had increased company exports to the Middle East

COURT IN THE ACT   as in 'courtroom'
                   caught

A spectator in court, who was there to see her boyfriend tried for a drugs offence, dropped a quantity of hashish from her handbag and was immediately arrested.

NOW YOU SEA IT ...   sea
                     see

A hotel on the edge of a cliff collapsed and was washed out to sea.

2 Students try to find homophones for the list of words. This is a good opportunity to revise the phonetic alphabet. Encourage students to use good monolingual dictionaries to check the pronunciation of any words they can think of.

Answers

four	–	for	wait	–	weight
made	–	maid	heal	–	heel
steal	–	steel	sight	–	site
been	–	bean	through	–	threw
peer	–	pier	stair	–	stare
rain	–	reign	tear	–	tier
sauce	–	source	night	–	knight
bread	–	bred	morning	–	mourning
sought	–	sort	blue	–	blew
meet	–	meat	lead	–	led

3 Students choose two or three homophones and invent an appropriate story to go with each one (this doesn't need to be written). They then decide on a headline using the homophone and when everybody is ready, read the headlines to the class. Students imagine what the story might be about.

Speaking: role play

Adequate time should be allowed for this role play as preparation and speech writing can be quite time-consuming. Make sure students have covered 'emphatic structures' before attempting this activity and remind them to use some of these structures in their speeches. It could be useful for feedback if the session is recorded.

1–3 Explain that each group is to choose one of the reports. They must then decide why their issue is the most deserving of the bequeathed money. (Omit one or more of the reports for a class with a limited number of students.) Each group should nominate a speaker and, when the speeches are prepared, a chairperson.

4–5 Remind students to use their feedback sheets during the meeting and to comment on strong as well as weak points. Rather than interrupt the speakers, students should make notes of any questions and put them to the speakers when the speeches have been given. It might be wise if at this stage the speakers are sitting with their groups so that help can be given with difficult questions.

6 When the session comes to an end tell the solicitor's representatives to decide who receives the money.

Writing skill: a formal report

Students write up a summary of the speeches and any decisions that were reached in the form of a report. This activity could be given for homework but students might benefit from working in groups first to decide on the main points in the speeches.

See **Language awareness: multi-word verbs (below)**

LANGUAGE AWARENESS: emphatic structures

1 Students examine the seven sentences and decide what they have in common.

Answer

All seven sentences have inversion of subject and object. Inversion has taken place because of:
- the negative or near-negative adverbs that begin the sentences
- the conditional structures 'should' and 'had' with 'if' omitted.

There are further examples of these structures in the Grammar Reference section which the students should refer to.

2 Students identify the stressed words in each sentence.

Answers

<u>Not only</u> has this Government reduced inflation, but unemployment has also <u>fallen</u>.
No <u>sooner</u> had I got in the bath than the <u>phone</u> rang.
<u>Rarely</u> does one find such fine examples of 17th Century furniture.
(No word is stressed)
<u>Only</u> when the power is off should you attempt to dismantle the machine.
On <u>no account</u> must you open this document.
<u>Had</u> we known the criminal's whereabouts we would have arrested him <u>sooner</u>.

Students write the sentences without inversion and compare the difference in terms of emphasis and levels of formality.

3 Students convert the remarks into formal statements that would appear in a letter.

Answers

a Rarely do I have customers with such an irresponsible attitude.
b Not only have you extended your overdraft, but you have also …
c No sooner had we finished our last meeting than you went away …
d Had I known about your other debts, I would have …
e Only when you have paid off your overdraft should you use your credit card.
f On no account should/must you use your credit card.
g Should you have any more financial problems …

4 Students rewrite the speech using the given structures and inverting subject and object. Allow for variations in speeches, provided that the structures have been used correctly.

Suggested answer

Good evening Ladies and Gentlemen. The attempted assassination of the Prime Minister this morning has shocked the nation. Rarely does one receive news of such a distressing nature. It showed a shocking disregard for human life. Had we been less fortunate, many innocent lives could have been lost. The people who commited this crime must be left in no doubt: not until those responsible have been severely punished will the nation be satisfied. The terrorists demand that we enter into discussions, yet so outraged are the population by this terrible act that we could not consider talking with these people. On no account will we give in to such pressure. Were we to weaken, the very foundations of our democratic system would be threatened.

5 To help them achieve correct pronunciation, students read the speech, banging their fists on the table at the points of stress marked.

Remind students to keep a record of formal structures in the Record Sheet on page 147.

LANGUAGE AWARENESS: multi-word verbs

1 Students decide on the idiomatic meanings of the multi-word verbs expressed in the cartoons.

Answers

> He couldn't get over the news: He couldn't
> believe it/come to terms with it.
> The thieves got away with it: They weren't
> caught.

2 Students now draw their own cartoons expressing
the literal meanings of the multi-word verbs in
the dictionary extracts.

3 It is important that students are at least aware of
the fact that not all multi-word verbs can be used
in the same way. This activity examines:

- multi-word verbs that require an object
- where the object must be in relation to the
  multi-word verb.

For an explanation of this students can refer to
the Grammar Reference on pages 173–4.

Answers

- Multi-word verbs like 'break down' and 'get
  away' do not take an object; 'get over' and
  'look after' do.
- Three-part multi-word verbs take an object
  and cannot be separated.
- The multi-word verbs can be separated in
  sentence f.
- When the multi-word verb is separated, the
  pronoun must come before the adverb.

4 Students complete the dialogue, replacing the
formal vocabulary with multi-word verbs. Remind
students to separate whenever possible.

Answers

> a get down to
> b got over
> c hand them out
> d fallen off
> e point something out
> f pass over
> g come up with

Remind students to keep a record of informal and
formal structures in the Record Sheet on page 147.

12 Crime and Punishment

PART ONE
Crime in society (SB page 134)

Lead-in

1 Students look through the list of crimes and discuss the questions about crime in their country. The distinction in the second question might help them in the ranking activity in Activity 2. Before holding the discussion, refer to the extension activity below.

Note the following terms:
Ram-raiding: Using a van or heavy vehicle to forcibly enter premises with the purpose of stealing goods
Joyriding: Stealing cars to drive for 'fun'

2–3 This can be dealt with as a ranking activity either within or between groups or both. The discussion can be made more task-based if the students try to get their colleagues to change their scores.

Extension activity
One student from each group refers back to page 23 and looks at the list of phrases used when agreeing and disagreeing. The student monitors the discussion and takes note of how well the others use these phrases. This monitoring is best carried out secretly to allow for a more natural discussion.

EXAM FOCUS: (Listening, Section D) identifying topic and speaker

1–2 This exercise can be carried out under exam conditions as there are no learner training exercises for this activity in the Student's Book. After listening a second time, students can be asked to list the words or phrases they heard that helped them identify the topic and speaker before answers are given.

Answers
1 1 Burglary
  2 Handling stolen goods
  3 Joyriding
  4 Violence against people
  5 Drug dealing

2 1 Concerned citizen
  2 Convicted criminal
  3 School teacher
  4 Policeman
  5 Teenager

See **Language awareness: perfect tenses (page 73)**

Exploring pronunciation: word families

A major source of pronunciation error for non-native speakers of English is caused by the fact that words derived from a base word (e.g. 'criminal' from 'crime') may have a different pronunciation. The difference may be one of vowel sound (i.e. short vowel and long vowel/diphthong),consonant sound (usually silent/non-silent letters depending on part of speech) or word stress (stress changing from one syllable to another).

1 Students work in pairs and decide on the pronunciation of the vowel sounds in the pairs of words.

Answers

Crime /aɪ/	Criminal /ɪ/
Moral /ə/	Morale /ɑː/
Human /ə/	Humane /eɪ/

2 This activity focuses on the change in pronunciation that often occurs within word families depending on whether the word is an adjective or a noun. Students supply the noun and decide on the pronunciation of the adjectives and the nouns.

Answers

Adjective		Noun	
clear	/ ɪə /	clarity	/ æ /
natural	/ æ /	nature	/ eɪ /
sane	/ eɪ /	sanity	/ æ /
vain	/ eɪ /	vanity	/ æ /
clean	/ i: /	cleanliness	/ e /

3 Students now examine the change in pronunciation between the verb and the noun of the same base word.

Answers

Noun		Verb	
adverti<u>s</u>ement	/ ɜ: / / s /	adverti<u>s</u>e	/ ə / / z /
ba<u>th</u>	/ a: / / θ /	ba<u>the</u>	/ eɪ / / ð /
brea<u>th</u>	/ e / / θ /	brea<u>the</u>	/ i: / / ð /
clo<u>th</u>	/ ɒ / / θ /	clo<u>the</u>	/ əʊ / / ð /
lo<u>ss</u>	/ ɒ / / s /	lo<u>se</u>	/ u: / / z /
redu<u>c</u>tion	/ ʌ / / k /	redu<u>c</u>e	/ ju: / / s /
<u>sig</u>n	/ aɪ / silent g	<u>sig</u>nal	/ ɪ / / g /
supervi<u>s</u>ion	/ ɪ / / ʒ /	supervi<u>s</u>e	/ aɪ / / z /

PART TWO
The right to smack

Lead-in

1 Put students into groups of three or four for this activity. Some of the punishments might include physical ones (you could, at this point, highlight the difference in severity between smacking and beating) or the withholding of privileges (pocket money, going out with friends).

2 Appoint a group leader who can then report the views of the group to the whole class. You could write the punishments on the board and see whether each group goes for a 'tough' or 'soft' approach in dealing with other people's children.

Reading technique: skimming

1 Set a time limit of around three minutes for this question. Students skim-read three texts, all from different sources, in order to choose the best title.

Answers

Text A d
Text B c
Text C a (although e is possible)

2 Activity 2 is fairly open-ended: make sure that students give adequate reasons for their choice of photo.

Possible answers

A Text A ('We'd all rather take care of "good" children')
B Text C ('He ... sped off, shouting a fricative word of abuse')
C Doesn't match any text because the woman appears to have lost the court case.
D Text A ('We'd all rather take care of "good" children') or Text B (A child minder 'She ... had been caring for Luke Formann')
E Doesn't match any text except possibly Text A

Reading technique: appreciating the style of a text

1 Students discuss the best stylistic descriptions for the texts. This activity requires closer examination of the texts.

Answers

Text A: persuasive, encouraging (actual source: booklet for parents, 'The No-Smacking Guide to Good Behaviour')

Text B: neutral, factual, objective, balanced (actual source: *The Independent*, front-page article)

Text C: exaggerated, cynical (actual source: *The Independent*, opinion article)

2 Students match further extracts with the texts they belong to. This provides further practice in examining the style of texts.

Answers

a Text A
b Text C
c Text C
d Text B
e Text A
f Text B

See Language awareness: articles (page 73)

Ask students what their reactions are to the story in Text B. Would such a story be likely to occur in their country? Students could work profitably in groups, generating ideas on the rights and wrongs of smacking young children. Refer students to the phrases used in the letters to newspapers on page 22. If possible, show students some examples of letters that have been written to 'quality' newspapers like *The Times*, *The Independent* or *The Guardian*.

1 Before students attempt the writing task they should look again at the section on emphatic structures on page 131. They can use these structures to state their point of view more forcefully.

2 In addition to the phrases in Unit 2, students can also incorporate some of these formal phrases in their letter.

PART THREE
Living in fear (SB page 139)

Lead-in

1 Discuss the issue of crime with students, encouraging them to relate any anecdotes about anybody they know who has been a victim of crime. Does a fear of crime in their country tend to be generated by media scare stories of particular crimes?

2 Students decide what they would do in each of the situations. Insist that this is done confidentially at this stage.

3 Students now try to guess what each of their colleagues would do in each of the situations. This can develop into quite a lengthy discussion as students justify their guesses based on their knowledge of their colleagues. It will also offer a good opportunity to monitor students' use of second conditionals.

4 Students discuss whether or not they feel nervous at home alone at night and list the precautions they would take to protect themselves from burglary or burglars. The visuals can be used as prompts.

This activity is best carried out in pairs and then groups, as it trains students to look out for structural clues to help them complete the cloze. This will be more constructive if they can share ideas.

1 Students read the text and the extracts first to get a general understanding. Encourage them to do this quite quickly and not to worry about any words they don't understand.

2 Students read the text and extracts a second time, taking note of any clues that will help them complete the cloze. Four clues have been given in the Student's Book as examples of what to look for.

Answers

'All is well': This is positive and contrasts with 'But what was that?'

'All is secure': This logically follows on from extract A which outlines the series of checks that the writer makes before she goes to bed.

'I watch television': This would logically come before 'When I must finally switch off.'

'I sit rigid in my bed': This must come towards the beginning of the text where the author describes her feelings in bed.

3 Students try to find similar clues in the rest of the text.

   E.g.   'One friend of mine.' – 'Another friend'
          'the wardrobe door' – 'Not only was the wardrobe a no-no'

When they have agreed on a final, completed version, students compare answers in groups or as a class. Allow them to justify their decisions first before giving answers.

Answers

  2 G
  4 D
  6 A
  8 C
10 F
12 B

Vocabulary development: dealing with unknown words

1
Answers

a tiptoe
b howling
c neurotic
d voracious
e straining

2 Allow about 15 minutes or so for students to work out their own definitions for the words listed. Don't let them use a dictionary until the final stage where they can check their intuition.

Listening technique: specific information

1 Ask students if they know what a Crime Prevention Officer is and whether they have ever heard of one of them in their own country. Ask them to list the kind of things a Crime Prevention Officer would advise people to do to avoid having their house burgled. They should refer to the picture for ideas.

2 Students listen to the talk and make notes of the advice given.

Answers

Lighting
Leave a light on when you go out, fit security lights to the outside of the house.

Windows
Downstairs windows provide easy access, upstairs windows can be reached by ladder or drainpipe. Check windows are locked at bedtime, even small windows. Fit window locks on the inside. Louvre windows are risky as glass can be removed, so if possible replace them.

Doors
Don't invite burglars in! Fit a chain or an eyehole (particularly elderly people), fit British Standard security locks to back doors and patio doors.

General advice
Fit a burglar alarm, don't approach an intruder at night, telephone the police.

Extension activity
Having listened to this advice, students can be asked to respond to the precautions the writer took in the text 'Home Alone'. To begin with, ask students to re-read the article and underline what they

consider to be sensible precautions and those they consider to be rather excessive. Using the information in the listening activity they can write a leaflet, 'Feeling secure in your house at night'. They should consider the potential audience, namely frightened individuals who might sometimes take excessive and perhaps dangerous precautions. (In the case of fire, what might happen if the wardrobe were against a bedroom door?)

LANGUAGE AWARENESS: perfect tenses

1 Students match the extracts with the appropriate time line.

Answers

1 e	4 b
2 g	5 f
3 a	6 c

2–3 Students read the newspaper article and circle all the examples of perfect tenses and then in pairs or groups discuss their uses

4 Students find and correct the statements with mistakes.

Answers

a Have you read this report on crime statistics yet?
b It's no wonder people have been worrying a lot about crime lately.
d Statistics for violent crime have improved/have been improving since 1987. Until then they were/had been a lot worse.
e Apparently, the crime rate was a lot lower 10 years ago.
f So far, cases of vandalism haven't risen much.
g They will be arresting a lot more people in 2010.
h I suppose they will have built a lot more prisons by 2010.
j By the time it's finished, the study will have taken 3 years.
k They'll have been collecting data for three years.

LANGUAGE AWARENESS: articles

1 Students examine the five groups of sentences and comment on the use or non-use of articles, finding the incorrect sentence in each trio.

Answers

The general view is that 'the' is specific and 'a' or no article is non-specific. This is true for most of the correct sentences. The following points should be highlighted, however:

- John's in prison/John's in the prison
  In the first, John is serving a sentence, in the second he is visiting.

- We usually use the definite article with expressions like 'play the guitar'.

- We often use the definite article when talking about science and technology (e.g. 'the telescope').

Incorrect sentences:
I don't like reading the books.
It's supposed to be worst prison in the country.
I'm looking for the good guitar. Do you sell them?
I'll get married one day but I don't think I'll have the children.
That's a telescope I was telling you about.

2 Students give examples from the sentences of general and specific nouns. If they have any problems, refer them to the Grammar Reference section which explains the apparent inconsistencies with the rule that 'a' or no article is non-specific.

Answers

General
Books are expensive.
John's in prison. (prison seen generally as an institution)
I've bought a guitar.
I'm learning to play the guitar. (this is not a specific guitar)
You shouldn't give children too much freedom.
You should give a child lots of love and attention.
The telescope was invented by Galileo. ('the' is not used here to specify a particular telescope)

Specific
The books are over there.
John's in the prison. (seen not as an institution 'generally' but a specific prison)
He put the telescope in the bedroom.

3 Students read the text and answer the questions.

Answers

'in school':
A common expression without an article (see 'in prison' above).

'the community':
The meaning is general but we often use the definite article when making reference to a communal body shared by us all.

'A boy on a bike', 'The boy on the bike':
The first is non-specific, the second specific.

'the human slalom':
Yes we have: 'shoppers'.

4 Students look for similar examples of 'a'/'the'/no article in the text.

5 Students supply the missing articles where required. In some cases more than answer is possible and students should be encouraged to discuss the different meanings.

Answers

A child minder has the right to smack children in her care, the High Court (*there is only one High Court*) ruled yesterday, renewing the fierce debate (*it must be known if it's renewing*) over corporal punishment. Anne Davis, over whom the test case (*the one just mentioned*) was fought, said it was a victory 'for every parent in the land (*England*) who believes in the reasonable use of physical discipline'. Mrs Davis, 34, who has three children, said it was a 'victory over the politically correct who cannot tell the difference between loving discipline and child abuse'. But the ruling brought instant demands from the National Society for the Prevention of Cruelty to Children and from the National Childminding Association for a change in the law to ban smacking by child minders. Local Authorities were alarmed by the comments of John Bowis, the junior health minister, who said, 'Clearly what the judgement has done is to underscore common sense'.

6 The difference between 'a junior health minister' and 'the junior health minister' is that in the first there is more than one, in the second there is only one.

Feedback – a chance for you to get involved!

We, the authors, hope that you have enjoyed using *Candidate for* CAE. We are keen to receive feedback from teachers and students and would therefore be extremely grateful if you could take a few minutes to respond to the following points:

Layout/organisation (Were the activities clearly labelled and easy to follow? Was the Contents map useful?)

Visuals (Were the visuals appropriate for your students? Were you able to exploit them for vocabulary purposes?)

Skills/exam preparation (Did the book have an appropriate balance of skills? Was the emphasis given to the exam sufficient for your students' needs?)

Timing (Was there sufficient material in each unit? How long did it take you to complete a unit on average?)

Learner Training (Did your students complete their review sheets? If so, did they need prompting from you? If not, why do you think they didn't?)

Additional comments

Please photocopy the form and send your comments to:

Fiona Joseph and Peter Travis
c/o The Editorial Department
Phoenix ELT
Campus 400
Maylands Avenue
Hemel Hempstead
Hertfordshire HP2 7EZ
England
Fax: +44 (0)1442 882151